T0149807

Critical Acclaim

THE PLEASURES OF
THIS PLANET AREN'T ENOUGH

THE PLEASURES OF
THIS PLANET AREN'T ENOUGH

by

Stedmond Pardy

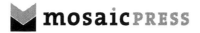

Library and Archives Canada Cataloguing in Publication

Title: The pleasures of this planet aren't enough / by Stedmond Pardy.

Other titles: Pleasures of this planet are not enough

Names: Pardy, Stedmond, 1983- author.

Description: Poems.

Identifiers: Canadiana (print) 20200377981
              Canadiana (ebook) 20200378031

ISBN 9781771615440 (softcover) ISBN 9781771615457 (PDF)
ISBN 9781771615464 (EPUB) ISBN 9781771615471 (Kindle)

Classification: LCC PS8631.A7415 P63 2020
                 DDC C811/.6—dc23

Published by Mosaic Press, Oakville, Ontario, Canada, 2020.
Second Print Edition, 2022.

MOSAIC PRESS, Publishers
www.Mosaic-Press.com
Copyright © Stedmond Pardy / Mosaic Press

Printed and bound in Canada. Reprinted 2023.

Cover Design by Andrea Tempesta

MOSAIC PRESS
1252 Speers Road, Units 1 & 2, Oakville, Ontario, L6L 5N9
(905) 825-2130 • info@mosaic-press.com • www.mosaic-press.com

Dedication

this book is dedicated to those who didn't think,
or want this to Happen, thank you

Acknowledgments

I would like to Thank Lori, Dawn, Wendy, Samantha, & Spencer Pardy, Merlin, Morvil, Warren, Jesse, Amanda, Stedmond Sean, Carlie, Aaron, Malik, Juliette & Warrick Manners. Kathleen Longboat, Brent & Carl Couckuyt, Marc Brown, Mikey Lewis, Dave Whang, Ana Vicente, Roy Chen, & Oliver Winerib, Forbeing sources of Light when things got "Dark". Big thanks to Nik Beat (RIP), the Lonely Vagabond, Brandon Pitts, Bede & Leo Mac, Daniel Goggin, & Reginald for Believing in my work, when I didn't, Sharon & Carl for the books that made me want to write (RIP). The best friend of my youth Dayne Barrett (RIP) Paul Mcdonald (RIP) Jordan Manners (RIP) Glenda Maddott (RIP) a Teacher who cared, who i, being too young, never got to properly thank. The Staff at Mosaic Press for giving me a chance. The artists whose work helped me change direction, & Last but not least, You, whoever you are, for reading this book.

I try to smuggle unto poetry what I want to Read & hear myself. What I feel is Missing in the medium, today. It has Gotten to be so Cliquey, & Hermetic. "Word poetry is for Every man, but soul poetry, alas, is not heavily distributed" said My poet hero. & I agree. I attempt to write stuff about whats happening In the world, & from my own personal experiences, Visions, & forebodings. That I hope could appeal to the Intellectual. But also to those people who don't read much poetry, & find readings to be …tedious. One that those with a knowledge of art history can appreciate, but those without it, can resonate with it as well. I'm self educated, so I consciously cultivated an unusual, Signature approach to the page & stage. Since I felt very alienated from the academic, & Slam Approaches. I had to try something else. I can't really articulate what I'm trying to do, As a poet. It's better you experience it & decide for your self.

Stedmond Pardy, November 2020

Contents

Crickets • 1

Last shift at "the Royal" • 3

A free jazz poem for Joan Baez • 5

A fragment of a Long poem written whilst walking down Yonge street • 9

Beached Whales 1 • 12

Azoth • 17

Ode to Liza Minnelli • 19

"The Combination of Salt, Mercury & Sulphur"• 25

E! True Lakeshore story • 28

The Search Warrant • 34

Edward Bernays/ "Bathtub gin" • 36

"A Lesson in Impermanence"• 38

Corners' Room • 40

The Apotheosis of Salvador Dali • 44

"The Script for Taxi Driver scared the shit out of Everybody" • 50

Travis Bickle goes to Hollywood (variations on the opening words
of Dante's "Inferno") • 53

Infant monkeys eating Aspartame/ "Cody Jarrett • 58

When Harry doesn't get his Laundry • 62

Gargling with Bleach • 65

5 shaded, black circles for Madama Butterfly • 68

Olga • 73

The Zodiacal year of the Metal Rat • 77

Sky Masterson • 80

For Lana Shields • 86

A Poem written on the day Lou Reed died • 89
CN Tower (a.k.a Sergeant Sarah Brown) • 93
Stairlifts • 96
Don Octavio DeFlores • 99
April 30th, 2020 •105
List of Poetry Readings and Essential Appearances by Stedmond Pardy •109
Biographical Note •113

Crickets

There's something slightly eerie about
Sitting like a sick, Monarch……. Ignored
By his physician …..
Picking at a fruit & fibre muffin, inside a
McDonalds, at 5:15 A.M, Nursing a small, black coffee, without
Any- sugar,
With only 40 dollars left to your
         Name
When You've spent the last 3 weeks sending out resumes
For the most degrading,
Muse crushing jobs, & only received- A
DEAD SILENCE
& You've sent your best poems out to various
Poetry mags, over the last, 9 months
& only heard
      - Crickets-

There is Something truly depressing, (I swear), about
Sitting in a McDonalds, at
     5:15 A.M,
Biting your nails because you're horrified! Terrified you might be
Developing Sleep apnea, **& l**osing
Your hair,
Praying for a passageway, a worm hole to another dimension to
Open up for you to-enter…. &
You're waiting for daily subway service to
Begin
So that you can crash upon the couch of some shrill, benevolent
-- HARPY ……

I'm telling you, Beloved Reader, Dear Comrade, there
Is something slightly scary about
Sitting
Like an ailing, Monarch ….. Deserted by his
           "Physician",
Picking at a fruit & fibre muffin
Inside an Empty, McDonalds, at
5:15 A.M
When the crescent moon, is still GLOWING in the
           Sky,
& you're nursing a small, black, coffee,   with
Out   any-   Sugar ……

Last Shift at "The Royal"

Projecting myself into a soundscape
    More Beautiful, than
Your ideal lovers
              Soul,
During my last 12 hour shift at "The Royal
Agricultural Winter
Fair",
I Stood, stroking the forehead
& Back!
Of a Tender, Black
Cow (The
Fairs Grand Champion)
As it licked (Poignantly) My Palm, & Wrist......

In the roaring silence of the late Saturday
    Night,
By Its cage, Vowing,
Never again, to gnaw! Bite! CHew,
..... DEVOUR,
Congealed ..... Fear, vowing,
(Quixotically)
 to be the unwav
-ering,
Undefeatable, Champion!! Of the
Veggie Burger,

The Robust! Charismatic Missionary
of,
BEEFLESS   Steak .....
Until,
A Passing, Drunken Farmer smirking,
Cruelly,
To himself, at the sight of

"US",

Informed me, that
My "New buddy", would be available
For purchase,
At my local Butcher, shop, or, super.......... market, By
The,
Start, Of
            The   week.

A Free Jazz poem for Joan Baez

It Feels as If I knew You
In a past Life,
You could have been My Sister,
Enemy, Lover, MOTHER, Girlfriend,
Ruler or Wife!
All I know is That You're Definitely
A kindred Spirit?
But I can't remember Us & Our Families
Dying From the Plague,
Us being Crucified upon the Most
Crooked-est of Crosses,
Whoring Ourselves on the Cobblestone
Streets of Mala Strana, Prague,
I don't Remember the LOVE &
Stimulating PAIN,
That We experienced outside The
Dali Museum in Figueres, Spain!
Witnessing the Tomato & Bullfights
Through the eyes of a Drugged
& Drunken babies Brain? Clayey
Labyrinthian coffin GREEN Chrysalis
BLACK,
The 1st, 2nd, & 3rd Diwalis
The Mysteries at Eleusis,
Facing the Firing Squad on a warm
Summer night walking A Radio
around a Strangled
Stick!
The Garden of Eden!

The Black Hooded Executioners
Shiney Axe!
At the Haunted Tower of London,
Concretizing Liquid?
WET LEATHER!
Our Katabasis-
...... Wordless Poems!
Us having blonde hair & Blue eyes,
While living In Helsingborg, SWEDEN!
The Torture chambers of Venice?
& The Middle East!
Us devouring bootlegged Liquor,
Gnawing Hallucinogenic Roots, & Berries!
Beaming Up
To an Inaccessible Land of Bergelmirs, Asuras,
Oceanids & Fairies!
While Picnicking in Central Park New York,
In the 1320's,
Hiding From The 'Pork',
Moments of Realization,
Really Divining
What's on the Other end of That Fork!
Me telling, You:

'If Anything were to happen To Me
Or If I was to Go!
Don't forget Me! Joan Baez,
Because Even If I was Trapped in
The Advanced stages of Alzheimers,
There's No way
I could Ever Forget about You'
& Our Time as
Dinosaurs! Leopards! Insects! Snakes! Birds!
Monkeys,
Pandas,
Foxes,
Sloths,
Elephants,

Butterflies! Penguins, Neanderthals,
Bacteria, Trees, & Fish! ? ? !
& The Extended Time we Spent,
As Coyote wolf hybrids, &… a Dying kids
Wish.

You can't even Remember Rogue Zoo Keepers
& Auschwitz! Mesopotamia!
The Floating World of Japan,
……When The 'Black Ships' Came!
The Rue Git Le Couer, AGARTHA,
Mist invading Our ravaged forests,
& 'The Exploding plastic Inevitable',
You can't even remember Red clouds! Orange
Skies! Silver waters, Black sand,
….Gold moons!
Us being lynched by the Klan,
Crossing the Bering strait!
Walking the plank, the Basement of Studio 54,
African tribal Drums whipping Us
& Our now extinct Tribe
Into Shamanic ecstasy!
At Celebrations of Pre-logical Existence,
Thelonious Monk, Schubert, Darlene Shrugg, The Viletones,
Duke Ellington, Robert Johnson,
The Stooges, The Doors, Buddy Bolden, & Sonic Youth
Live in the Flesh, Brandon Pitts! Nik Beat! Bede & Leo Mac,
The Lonely Vagabond,
& The Renaissance of The 2200's,
The Resistance!
The Human Be-in of 1967,
Pink Floyd's 'Games for May',
& That Awkward Life when I was
The Woman! & You Were
The MAN -
We've existed as casualties of the Subhuman
Psyche since the Very Beginning of The Idea
Of   Time!

I have already Squandered the Platinum
Of Our Youth in THIS Life,
What do You Think I'm Going to Do
To the Blood diamonds of Our future?

Ah, I can clearly remember The
Nebulous Vistas of Our lunar earth!
Us
Self exiling Ourselves along the
Seashores of That OTHER   World,
Studying The Heraldry of 'Finfolk'?
David Bowie & Nine Inch Nails Touring
Together in 1995,
The St. John, St. Vitus Dancing Mania
Of 1518,
You dating Steve Jobs? & Bob Dylan,
& You locking arms with Me,
After
Your   performance, at Roy Thomson
 HALL.

A Fragment of a Long poem written, whilst walking down Yonge Street

...Ah, Toronto! My "Bereaved
Marie"?
I loved You, ONCE, I loved you like Woody Allen
Loved "Manhattan",
O, Yonge Street! I can't say I hold that same sentiment
Today,
We were of "One Flesh" ....once,
When I strolled up & down you when I was younger
"Heaven was TRULY Mine", Heaven for ME, was
To be found in the very midst, of-
You,
Some of My fondest memories! Some
Of my Fondest, Most cherished memories
Are of the times I skipped/ cut
class, & wandered around You by myself
Like Diogenes with
His lantern lit in the daytime in search
Of an HONEST man,
With only My allowance or hoarded Christmas
& Birthday money in my
Pocket,
Sometimes if I was lucky, maybe even a, joint,
Like I said,
Heaven seemed mine! Back then,
With all the people new to my Rookie eyes,
The stores, the restaurants, Bars, & the scents,
Made all the more sweet by the

Fact that I wasn't "technically" allowed
To be downtown by, myself, I
Felt like a Nazi looted, Matisse! & a headless, Angel!
Without Wings back then, Yonge street, I felt an Emotion that is
Actually impossible to
Define!
Is it truly "Better to be King for a Night,
Then a schmuck for a lifetime"?
"The King of Comedy", for Me, is one of the greatest Black
Comedies of, all time! Have you seen
It?
In Your Cruel, moist, indifferent Palm, I commended my eternal, Spirit!
Now the Pleasures of this Planet, aren't enough?
I was alone back then, Yonge street,
As I mentioned, I am Alone right now,
Although,
I don't WANT to Be,
Should I see a Psychic? I've already
Passed 3!
What will You look like in 2063?
What Robust, exhilarating Joy would have been mine, despite the fact
That I'm Coloured,
If I could
Have strolled down you in the year 19
23?
If Quantum theorists are right,
Then everyone who has ever walked down THIS Street,
& everyone who will EVER walk down this, Street,
Is walking down this Street holding my
Skeletal hand right
NOW!
The sky is a brilliant baby Blue, without, a single
Cloud,
The Black, lactating Sun is rising to its, ZENITH,
My Mindscape, is full of stubby arms reaching out of the
Cement, grasping for the charred Skeletons, of the
Constellations of..... Stars.

Shut the Fuck, UP!! Yonge street,
"JIHAD ME AT HELLO",
That was actually the ridiculous Headline, that greeted
Me on the cover of Todays paper,
I'm not making this
Up,
I am living, I have lived, I live like a Deposed, King,
& a........ BEACHED WHALE,
My glittering throat, blazed like "The berry of solace", & a
Trinket of
Joy
Ah, Yonge street!
I just passed an Aggressive panhandler hoisting up a card
Board sign that says
"Need Money For?"
& I wonder how much money he'll, get,
At the end of the
Day!!
What the Hell is with all the upcoming condos?
What the fuck did you do, to "THE BIG SLICE"?
"Elliots"& "Hmv"?
Why,
Why are you dolling yourself up, like a
Cut rate Times Square?
It's 2019! "'Tis the April of our prime",
& I'm just strutting down the World's LOOOOO
OOOOOOONG-est
Street!

Which just happens to, be....... You.

Beached Whales Part 1

1.Me.

Aboard that packed subway train at rush hour
I was the very, portrait, of
Dissociative, CALM, But on the inside, I,
......Cried!!

"A

Hang glider got struck by a streaking meteorite on
The Morning after the night, before, I met, you!! On
The Morning after the night before I met, you!
I was spiritually conjoined to a Chinese boy,
A Chinese boy
Whose eyes were gouged out by His beloved Aunt, I
WAS ALTERED FOREVER!! Just before I met, you, Baptized, Anew,
Altered forever! By the intuitive hunch that I would find you,
Doggie paddling in the scarred in every way by me sky
Of skulls smuggling un
Wanted vegetation to those of us living in
Blazing sweatshops transfigured into
A lone ziggurat of melting ice, yelling, "Come!
Come & take a lick of one, of our...cones!?
"Come, Let us march against the powers of heaven,
And set black streamers in the firmament,
To signify the slaughter of the gods"
Come!! Come strum your acoustic weapons,
All OVER our Electric country! This music,
Makes our legs, feel like a field, of,
WHEAT?

But a disfigured World War 4 veteran, & an
Underappreciated woman discover true
Love! Beauty,
& a Magical transformation,
After moving into a small cabin, on our
Sprawling, estate! But, The!!
But, The!?
But the Pixelated pictures, on your laptop screen!!
The Earthling Outside, Reality. The
Man who fell to, EARTH,
.... Counting.......
Stars,
Altered forever, by a replenishing infection that
Hospitalized a glamorously destitute couple,
Snow shoe-ing across
The prairies in the late summer with a blissful,
Socially unorthodox,
Hypersensitive, wastrel with a FASCINATING personality,
On the Morning after the night, before
I met, you.

On the Morning after the, night, Before I met, you.
Crazy Horses warriors fought their
Last major battle at Wolf Moun-
A Bank robbery suspect was captured after
He posted a picture of himself holding
A Star trek Klingon sword,,
& a submachine gun on -Instagram- before
Pulling a violent hei-
The RCMP was probing serious new allegations of
Illegal lobbying by a former advisor to Canadian
Prime Minis-
Roaming gangs of Chihuahuas were
Terrorizing the streets in Ariz-
20 People were stabbed at a high school in
Pi-
Squeezed by the worst ever drought
In the States' history,

California was dying of thirst & gr- A Snow sto-
A timid Spermatozoon was nervously
Awaiting Ejacula-
A stupid chick more useless than parents who
Can't cook was arrested in Texas for
Dial-ing 911 repeatedly because
She ran out of Cigare- Wednesdays
Unofficial pick 6 lottery
Numbers were: 24, 12, 69- & a sea lion
That befriended a rustic youth with Aspergers syndrome
Was happier than
Over protective Russian, Italian, Arabic, Irish, Scottish! Indigenous,
& Zionist Fathers finding out that their
Favourite!
Most doted upon Daughter is marrying some,
African …Canadian!
Or.… Mulatto Dude interrogating Socrates beyond
Our Solar, system,
Probing the furthest reaches of,
Interior space, when my mustangs, ALMOST got
Turned,
Into- DOG FOOD,
On the Morning after the Night-
On the Morning after, The-
On the Morning after the Night, before, I
Met,   You".

2. You.

Aboard that packed subway train at Rush hour,
Your face betrayed not one, single emotion, but
In your 4-d, printed......Head, You
--Said:

"Sectarian Death squads!
Wandering the desserted desert Of a Crack heads pipe dream,
Who can turn vinegar into your favourite wine,

& contaminated water, into
Champagne, I can transform your ewwwws, into AWWWWS
Like a strong, Germanic
King,
For you I'll Survive being -taken for a ride-
By a Burly Calabrian hitman, with piercing
Grey, blue eyes,
EYES,
Jet black hair, & a high pitched falsetto,
For You I will Race, sprint through a swarm, of enraged, African bees,
Bees, & emerge unstung for, You,
For You, I will superglue my stacked deck of upturned cards
Onto every smashed glass, table, &
Wear my liquid skeleton outside of my soft, skin, like a
Twin crab scuttling indirectly toward it's goal,
Which lays directly ahead of, it, I'll-
I'll rip off your Blind fold made of
Wool, & remove the muzzle from your mouth,
& tear up the Stale book of old rules, For you,
I'LL FREE THE IMPRISONED GOLDSMITH,
& Cook every Sacred Cow, & Golden Goose,
& Wake the sleeping giant, & Dogs,
Where they lay, (if I must)
& bear witness to the pen-Ultimate truth,
& Beat a few Kenyans, & Ethiopians,
in a long distance marathon,
For You, I will Face the Discordant music, &
Evade the Disso-lution, For…. you,
I'll confide my secret belief
That when Salvador Dali died, he became again our, supreme
Ruling deity,
Which explains why the world, is, the way it now, is,
For You, I will shine a Harsh! Unbearable light upon everything
That has ever been lost! & Forbidden! Bidden. Burnt! Burnt,
Hidden, & Reveal The, Hoarded,
Esoteric wisdom of the ages!! & Unbag,
the legendary cat,
I will Shed the white blood of my soul to give you

The skeleton key, & the whole,
Unexpurgated hog!
I will risk life! LIFE<Limb! Limb, Love! LOVE,
Sanity! Poverty, Health,
& Reputation, & pay the STEEP, price, in order to grant you
A Precognitive, glimpse, A mechanical, Bald eagle's eye view, of The
Things to, come, & Conjure -something,-
New,
You have Noooooo, idea!
What I'm willing to put my nervous system through,
The perilous Journeys!
Of Enoch! Dante! Odysseus? Kevin Garvey,
& Every romantic! Swash buckling Hero,
& Human headed, bird,
Bringing us the
Broomstick of the wicked witch of the west,
Can't hold a snuffed, bloody, Candle!!
To what I'VVVE been, through!!
& will continue, to go
Through,
To earn your-Love!! LOVE, &
 Conjure, SOMETHING,

New"

Azoth

"WE'VE fought the WRONG, people!"

& Now the florescent red sculpture of an emotionally
Volatile dog is "Pouncing" out
of the sand, of an Inner city playground,
& Genetically modified, mosquitoes! Are
Being released into
The Wild…

"We've fough-! We
Fought! The WRONGGGGGG, people, &
"Binges can harm young brains", We fought!
The WRONG people.

& Now the Dominatrix of my hysterical, thoughts, rules
Our world, with an IRON HAND, inside a mink,
Glove,
& a Russian scientist,

        Re-
Weaving us back into the fabric of a building
Destroyed by a, Rocket, in
The eastern Ukraine, spots, a mountain sized, meteorite,
Heading,
    OUR way.

We've fought! The WRONGGGGGGGGGG
-GG,
Fucking people, I Say !!?

& Now, we've collectively FORGOT how to keep the
Parasitic gluttons, away,
From the Blossom, A
Drunken, department store Santa Claus, staggering
Down the lonely street, is "Bringing us all our heart's Desire",
& Now a
Terrifying monster, made of Un
-cooked processed… Meat,
Near that mirrored, Venusian, lake, & "The Great proscenium",
Chases me   in   your
DREAM(S),

"Every 15 minutes, of   The Day"……

Ode to Liza Minnelli

I Spray paint your image on the
Graffiti mural'd walls
Between Dundas West & Keele
Subway stations, as a
"Red Headed Beggar Girl" crawling towards
Me on your knees,
Against the backdrop of the
Copper
Metal
Chasm?
…. With my black eye liner I draw you
As a crude stick figure on the
Smudged up mirror, of a
Filthy public washroom,
I finger paint you as the
Forbidden modern primitive!
Wintering a tropical soundscape of my heart,
I scribble You in gold & silver & violet crayon on
A pink piece of construction
Paper,
& Magnet it on my parents refrigerator,
& wonder if they REALLY
Like it?
"There is no chosen race in Nature"
…..The droppings of last weeks' trip out
Are still scattered upon our floor,
You stand, Sandwiched alone here, WHOLE!
In a divided kingdom between

Heaven & Earth! Death,
& re-birth!
Ready to flee away from me
With Shelley's "West Wind", you stand!
Knowing
That "the elements in modern society
Destructive of the best qualities
Of human nature"
Have been laid out mercilessly
For our insatiable eyes
Countless times, you stand!!
Hands on hips, knowing that the wise
Words
Of the greatest souls who have passed
Through this terrifying
Place!
Have fallen upon deaf ears,
You stand for 30 years!! Where only the
Holy Ghost shall
                Shall come upon thee,
All the infinite beasts of the feral fields
Yield to ye!
She of the Serpent Woven skirt!
Your tattered robe is my whole fucking world!
& I'm dying to see you shake it off-
You are "Something words could only caricature & diminish",
I can't help but masturbate,
Watching
You make love to life!
I look at you young Liza Minnelli, & I see my DESTINY,
My future... I think?
You're the lode star!
& Doomed salvation,
The Aromatic essence of green blood
Red people smell when dead birds start
Falling from the sky-
The incommunicable pain soothing
Transcendent Bliss,

The attack of the Hunch backed creep!
The Random attack of the nit picking
Couch Potatoes-
The attack of the Self injurers,
The Attack of the Superrrrr effeminate
Misogynists kissing at Picnic tables to the EWWWWWWWWWWWWW
WWW
WS'
Of spectators gathered, which may, or
May not,
Include ME!?
Massacre-er of liberty, & children's Toys!
Let's impregnate the distorted music
Of complete silence
With a single collaborative word, "Let us
Go where the omens of the gods &
The crimes of our enemies summon us!
THE DIE IS NOW CAST"!
Let's solve "The Mystery of the Leaping Fish"
With that fiend
COKE ENNYDAY!
Let's defile our chapped lips with
The cold soul of a defenceless
Creature!
Let's commit Harakiri, & do a
Hart Crane!

A timid painters aggressive brush strokes!
Interesting eccentrics from whom
You can't
Remove your eyes-eyes!
Looky here, LIZA,
I'm just a really lost guy stuck
Between the beginning & the end! Of
A highly flammable good time,
I'm just a melancholy star dancing
Across the sky
Of your new hotel room, the forsaken

Heralds radiant cry!
I'm just the moody daughter of promiscuous
Intimacies, & Retro charm!
I'm telling you about myself! …. Are you listening?
I enjoy Lawlessness!
Earthquakes! Boneless bodies, Ketamine!!
Marijuana kleenex?
Majestic performers Self destructing
On the stage, like ME,
& BULGING brides crueller than
Some asshole kicking a pregnant,
5 bodied dog!
Dog!
Unveiled monuments, monuments,
& widespread disease,
I feel that nothing could ever culminate
In great tribulations,
We are only now in the Genesis
Of our unrequited love,
Love!
I can't wait until we hit the "Book of Revelations"!
My father never gave up on a fig tree!
"Mute inglorious Hitlers",
I came to you in search of the
Perfect winter BOOT!
But found instead, a summer
Sandal,
I came to unannounce Jehovah's kingdom!
…wilt thou help me?
You see how I can now bring the poem
Back from its un-restless wanderings,
To exactly where it's supposed to
Be?
-Everything is moving stop
Motion-
You have NO fucking, EQUAL!
To YOU dear girl, there

Can NEVER!! Be a, sequel,
Our smoldering FIRE!
Can ne'er cool to a fine ash,
RUTHLESS TYRANT,
The very IDEAS of what it once
Meant to be women & Men have been
Dramatically altered!
What it means to be a "Human being"
Is Next!?
"Would it be permissible for a
Miseducated alien to try the
Truth & beauty pill"?
Old age is savagely Beating,
Beating! BEATING!!!
Our fleeting beauty & youth,
To a bloody pulp!
So we must make haste,
Because we're all innocent little children,
Infested with microscopic bugs!
Being molested,
By the perverted hands of Time!
O! The crude violent colors!
"The horrible honest toil",
Hark! The hot cubicles of diseased Pepper!!
"Alas! The hopeless wretches"!
Can our broken snowflakes still get hung?
Must the bewildered music of the bruised
Articulate oboe always
Get smeared
By
Grotesque monotone,
Liza?
Must you always remember the
Unforgettable times you opened up
Your audacious,
Permanently sealed mouth to
speak!

& a million different exotic birds
Flew out?
Must our Samson always get Seized,
By the philistines,
Like gondolas in the WIND?

"The Combination of Salt, Mercury, & Sulphur"

Every 15 Minutes of the Day the
Forest green beams of the 14 moons
     Of Neptune
Tousle My dry! & Damaged, DisHeveleD,
Eternally dandruff ridden, hair,
Sometime in the month of June during
The year, 3018!!
        I .....Mean,

AUGMENTED fourths!
   Fourths,
        FLATTED, fifths?
Icicles falling off of, Plant covered

       Condos,
Unpinned grenades of requited love
& unparalleled joy, untethered! un, canned!
       "un
Loosed" where Our pastures are
Everything but, Forest.....Green! I!!
Mean,
..... "East of Eden", & "West of
Zanzibar", on, "This side of Paradise",

In an Ornate, gilt frame, in the
Deep shadows of Skyscrapers!
.... "In many avanished Year & age" "RANGED

THUS FOR BATTLE ON THE
SACRED PLAIN".....In a world
Full of strangers ......
A Giant crack opens up in the Earth,
& a 12 headed,
Pre-adamic sculpture, Frees, itself, from
An oblivion, of,
                 Marble ......

Every 15 Minutes of the Day!
Day.

Your unmanned Predator drone spy planes, Mount
The foggy horizon, over

My camps of intern
-ment.

& Our ONE head, contains SIX faces,
"a Sunny Destination awaits You"?
& a colony of ants Lay siege! To
Your neighbours house
.....Every 15 minutes of the Day,
Every 15 minutes of the, Day!
Another dweeb,
Takes the ALS, ice bucket challenge
Every hour of the Night! In Paris, an Incognito American
Porn star is wooed by a "Penniless French Aristocrat"?
.....Every 15 Minutes of the Day.

Every 15 Minutes of the
Day, Day!
Some Genius is Locking either their Toddler,
Or Horribly Trained pets in a
HOT, un
Air conditioned Car, & a
Mute banshee, attempts to scream Blue,
Murder, or!

"SOMETHING TO, LIVE
FOR".......

Rescuers, end Searching for the wreckage, of
Our derelict Russian, cruise ship, at the Bottom
Of,
Lake Ontario,
As an Unbelievable Rumour!! "Congeals", into
An incontestable, fact!!

Every 15 Minutes, of......
The Day.

E! True Lakeshore Story

"What happened to America has happened to
him—the two were inseparable', Like the wind to the
sky "
   Gregory Corso In "Feelings Elegiac American"

You are the quintessential symbol of
"Modern Times" & society to me!
What has occurred in you, Dear comrade,
Is transpiring in our world!
I "Sar" you! Hunched over, strung out,
Sitting temporarily defeated
On that curb in front of the Laundromat,
Staring off into the aether, with that unseeing,
Ten thousand yard stare, that I myself know well,
In the early Toronto afternoon,
Your glassy eyes all teary, your glassy eyes,
That are heartbreakingly blue,
That had somehow managed to maintain,
The childlike innocence,
That the rest of your being, VISIBLY
Could not.

As I made my approach,
I thought to myself-
"I shall lift this Fallen woman!
I shall ennoble her! Only I, only I can
Teach her about the cruise ship disasters,
& the virgin soil epidemic!

Nobody else can help her!
Her friends & family are even more fucked
Up than she is! Is,
Degenerate drug addiction hereditary!? Is,
She going to Svengali me into the EXACT
Same thing that she will one day
Condemn me for!? Is,
THE PARTY REALLY OVER?
Because this is only the beginning of the
Drought! Doomed Salvation,
BEACHED WHALES!?
Her overwhelming presence will eclipse
Everything else (except poetry)
From my distracted view,
Every afternoon I spend with this broad
Will be
Like Christmas morning! &
Every night will be the dawning of a
New year!
Even though 15 years or so have past,
Since I last heard Kali singing her sighs,
Through the falling leaves of
A bird crowned tree!
15 years or so,
Since she & me have seen each other last,
I can't ignore her!
I shall restore her BEYOND her
Prior magnificence,
With the raised arms of the caryatid I will elevate
Her past her former glory!
& If I fail in this ridiculous, fucked up quest, I will let her
Drag me down into her own personal Hades!!
Where we'll live our sodden
Lives in Technicolor!
& Rob her Vampiric dealer pimps
House!
& Then shoot our way to the top of bop

City?
& Then HAND, in, HAND, we'll RUTHLESSLY trod!
A Self destructive path that even the most
Depraved of junkies would have thought "impossible"
To have, trodden!
How poetic! How triumphant! How
Gnarly, Quixotic, FRIGHTENING, & like
"The Twilight Zone" would all of that be!??
I will be the decaying victim of a mafia
Hit, & she
Will be the hitmans Cadillac trunk"!
… For some reason I pictured You, & ME,
Stranded on that "Slow boat to China",
………Lost at Sea.

When I introduced myself,
You turned around, suspiciously!
But when you realized who it was
You looked up glowingly at me, the seediest of smiles,
& I noticed scabby, needle marked
Chest & arms,
I saw brown, black teeth! One of the
Front ones missing-
I noticed that your partially scratched off
Nail polish was METALLIC BLUE!
I observed the garbage littered grass of the park,
Invertebrate thugs, joggers, cars, an injured rare lynx,
Bikes, "grinders", Families!
The outside air reeked of a Dolphin stampede,
I recognized! I noticed like I did
When I was an untarnished kid the
Innumerable shapes of the cirrus clouds in the
Splintered coffin! Of that reprehensible sky,
Pathetically, out of shock, Dear comrade,
I could hardly look you in the eye,
I was too spooked!
I falsely realized, who am I to save

Anyone! Especially you, I ain't no catch myself,
The handsome face of that introverted boy
You once knew, & admired,
Has hardened into that of an ugly man!

PLUS, I'm Balls DEEP!!!
In the syphilitic cunt of life, too!
Only I'm not lodged up in it, as
Nastily as you,
I don't drive or own a car!
I can't TAKE you to the drive in,
Or Lovers' lane!
Although, if you were fixed up just a little bit,
I'd DEFINITELY want to! Dear comrade,
Smash wolf swans ever written?
GHOST LETTER CHANCES? ...... Pitchfork Genius!!

I won't ever possess the paper Fools gold
To help you whiten the teeth,
That the chain smoke of cigarettes, heroin,
Speed, & Crack!
Have now turned brownish, black!
I can't apply lotion to your sunburnt soul!
The biker gang fugitive arrested for funeral slayings,
& the motion of matter!
Has scattered us into a different pattern,
You are the absent mother of three-
I can't abduct you from your Olmec-ian
Scene- I can see an ancient,
Orgasm-ing woman dying whilst lavishing birth
Unto an invisible, unfathomable,
Electronic force gorge-ing itself upon
The collected energy
Of every cities synthetic brain......
My luxurious bed is somebody else's Couch!!
& Regrettably, there's not room for TWO,
SOMETIMES THERE'S BUGS ON THE FLOOR!

A while ago after I renounced dealing the
Goods?
I took a vow of voluntary poverty,
"I am not interested in money,
I just want to be wonderful"!
Marilyn Monroe said something like that once
Dear comrade, & now I'm sharing it with you,
Although, I have only the slightest idea
WHY-
...There were 2 million things I could
Have done with you, but shamefully,
out of my Former cowardice. I did not ONE!
Your Dealer/pimp & his microbes were waiting
Across the street, & you appeared to be
Itching to rendezvous with them..... I THINK,
& my dad was going to be arriving soon,
So I let you go, whistling "AUTUMN LEAVES",
& "MEIN HERR".....
Last I heard one of your johns smashed
A glass bottle in your once stunning face,
Melted candle, answered prayer
........Cruel fate

Before we parted ways, you unspokenly
Said the following words that will
Always haunt me!
You telepathically hissed them at me as if
You were a Dragon!
You hissed the following haunting words
At me as if you were the Lady Pendragon
In "THE DIARY OF A DRUG FIEND"
By Aleister Crowley,
You hissed: "If our short lives are only supposed
To be a dream, Stedmond,
I wish someone would wake me up!
If my life is supposed to be a
Vicious, sweet, snuff film being screened
In some Divine the-a-tre,

In which the only Warhol-ian star is
ME!
Then tell the indifferent powers that be.....

To Please
TURN OFF THE PROJECTOR".

The Search Warrant

Just as "They" were about to kick in, our
Gilded bronze, door.

A figment of your imagination, caressed
My arm,
& a shaft of faint white, un-onion skinning light, drifted, across
Our dark, shadow,
While Heavy, computer generated winds, Swept across
Germany.

A Mute banshee, &
The Poisoned Eagle, SCREAMED,
& Fires were BURNING, in that Ocean, of,
GLASS.

In the beehives, & Anthills of Dehumanizing
Cement,
A Young male opera singer dressed,
In all black,
Paint splattered clothes, was busking on the corner....
"One universal Spirit", manifested itself, through ALL things,
& Unborn children, making hookers, Murderers! Sailors! Truckers,
& Politicians
Blush,
Were "lost, in a mutual, Dream".
....I was on your uncarpeted
Floor, about to open up, a Jewelled,
Pearl encrusted snuff box, full, full
Of Our favourite Anesthetic, You-

You were snuggled up beside me,
About to put on Bowie's
"Warszawa".

A quadruple rainbow, stretchedddddd, across, A
Carnivorus,
Sky,
Our Black sheep, was about to get wrapped,
Wrapped In, The Golden,
FLEECE,

& a smooth coated otter, & "Indias ONLY ape", took
Their first
"tentative steps", into the restorative,

Brown water.

Just! As "they" were about to kick,
IN,

Our Gilded   Bronze,

Door.

Edward Bernays/ "Bathtub Gin"

The stink of old
Blood,
& BBQ'd Raspberries, & Burnt steak! Are
Askewly
        Aswarm
With elderly Delinquent
Gangs
Of gentle skin head punks baby
Sitting children,
That have never even been Born!
Who frequent My favourite bars,
& Chase our hydrocodone
Dragon, around & around &
Around, & around, & around, & around in
Circles, with their Stuffed up, Noses?
Squinting troubled looks,
REALLY troubled–
"They may stretch Our necks on all
The gibbets in the land,
They may turn every rock into a
Scaffold– Every tree into a Gallows,
Every home into a grave, & Yet
The words on that parchment can
Never die! They may pour our blood on a thousand
Scaffolds, & Yet from every drop that dyes the axe a
New champion of freedom will spring into
Birth"! Looks,
As if to, Say!
"The Things above are Reflected

in the Things
Below"

Even tho- Even though we KNOW that one organ
Donor can save 8 lives, & that there are many
Different Obstacle'd! Forked, paths,
Usherette-ing Us ALL, the Same, WAY!!
To the dive bars patrons, "They", convey..... War! Psychic,
Toxins!
Pandemonium! ..... KARMA,
"Ruptured Enbridge tar sands Pipeline",
Tiny Helicopters Piloted by Human Thought!
Edward Bernays?
"Problem-Reaction-Solution"
Déjà vu!
The Flouridation of, Our, Radioactive Water- "The
9 places we never remember to put sunscreen"-
"The 6 places Dentists check most", Liberating Oppressors,
Expired Candy? Planned Obsolescence,
Weather Manipulation &, Transition/
DEATH!!!
Through the Mythical Medium
Of, Interpretive Dance....
As "I", Impressed, d,d,d,d,d, Con-f-use-d, In-trigu-ed, & .... Etc,
Order "YET" another
"Guinness",
At "The Texas Moon Café", on
Ossington & Queen, Ossington, &, Queen,
& try to decipher,
What exactly, 'TWAS, that
Pythagoras & His, followers,
Had against,

BEANS?

"A Lesson in Impermanence"

We met on New years Eve!

We met on New years Eve! Which
Was the day I got cast out
Of the place I was "then" Living,
(After I dropped a hit of acid at the "U.S Girls"!
"Zacht Automaat" show at
"Double Double
 Land")
& right away, We knew,
That some force far larger than
Ourselves,
Was pushing us, Pushing, "US"
Together.

"Thank You! For a lovely, &
Passionate evening! ..Sweet Dreams".

Within those few, Criminally brief hours We
Had the rare privilege of Spending
Together,
We managed to forge a connection deeper
Than 4 couples who sleep in separate beds
Could manage, in the span of 2,
or 3 years, didn't WE?

No matte-
No matter what vile, or golden, platinum
Plated fate, awaits me, in the future. I will always

Remember, Your flask of
Irish whiskey, & your Thermos, full of
Bathtub gin. Your Lost, earring, The
Bottle of, "prosecco", We
Shared,

& the genuine magic, that transpired between us
in the screening room, of that Madman, theatre,
& that booth, at "the Pint house",
The scent of your perfume,
...... Everything We discussed,
The way you rearranged My leopard print,
Scarf!
The way you rearranged my leopard print, scarf!
& the way, you-
& the way you kissed me for what
May have been, the last—Time.
As you were about to step onto the surprisingly
Emptied,
Streetcar, on that cold, immortal night
&, said:

"Thank you for a lovely & Passionate
Evening! Sweet Dreams!!! I Miss,
YOUUUU
UUU
U

...Already".

Corners' Room

I become an
        Agoraphobic!
As the term
Is misunderstood to
        Be, whenever I barge into your
Intimate,
Windowless, Anchorite like
      room,
& am crippled by social anxiety, whenever I
Dare leave
      it,

Your room is God! The Devil! The Virgin Mary, &
Jesus all smooshed into a fresh
    disease, turning
My red coke cans,
        White! & Our oranges,
GREEN?
Your Room is the elevator to the gallows! I tell, you, a
Lift to the
    Noose!!
..... An escalator to the.... stars, a muddy
Labyrinth of cra
       -cked dusty
Mirrors, in which
I
Recline, thinking lust filled- thoughts! &
Sob involuntarily!   Your
      Room,

Is a Slowly gestating fetus's
Cartilage, HARDEN-ing
Into BONE, & a Drug filled, Football!
Lobbed, into a Detroit
Prison-

"User descriptions!! Of the K
-Hole often include,
Vivid hallucinations, & distortions in, or complete
Loss
Of bodily awareness, sensations
of, floating,
flying!
Euphoria! & total loss of the perception of
-Time, users may experience worlds,
or dimensions
That are Indescribable,
All the
while,
Being completely unaware of, or having lost their
Individual identities, & their sense of an Ex
-ternal World". Your
Room!
Allows me to enter a WORLD, more fantastical,
Than even the most intense "K-Hole"
Can, your
Room is a presidential palace in -
Cairo!!
& a white blood cell in somebody else's
Body, An essential
Cog, in every Machine,
YOUR ROOM IS "NON LIQUID WATER BURIED
DEEP WITHIN THE EARTH'S CRUST"!
The Falling, brittle leaves, of
A Bird crowned
Tree!
"The best grandma anyone could
Ever ask

for!"
"The Athens of Cuba!" " A 148 pound, gadgetry encrusted
Exoskeleton" like
MINE,
Toronto's oldest Mexican
Restaurant? & a gulp of blood,
A cave of WONDERS, It's
The Curvature of...... space! The worst place,
To get a paper
Cut, The most cathartic, X-rated movie,
To ever win an Academy Award?
& The "World's Deadliest intersection".

The discovery of the approximate age of the
Earth's
Moon-
A Mystery,
That the most learned Theologians, Scientists, & Quantum
Physicists can't explain, your room contains 10 of the World's Most
Jaw dropping views!
Your room, is
The projection of the archetype of the Chinese
Symbol of ETERNITY,
The
Greatest amusement park!! For summer
Thrills,
A Multivehicle collision! "The Outer Limits", "THE
TWILIGHT ZONE", for Christ
sakes!
A Fortunate isle of the Blest, upon which we frolic
With our lost
Heroes,

The moment!

The moment we get them to moan "DON'T
STOP"!! .... "Don't
Stop",

Is the PRECISE moment that We FINISH??!
It's the prettiest nose in Brooklyn,
& The "Double Room", of which Baudelaire spoke,
"A Room, a truly spiritual Room",
                    A ROOM,
That is more like a
.... Dream,

It's a "Slow boat to China",
An Alternative Universe, in which we nightly,   sHaTtEr
The 6th
          wall.

          Your pigsty of a room is a small town
 Trollop!
Changing the ill Starred fate, of a delectable miscreant,
Sleeping his way to the top of the
                Heap,
After she displayed for him the errors,   of
His former- way,

The Nearly invisible, interactive home
Gym of
Your Intimate!!
          Windowless, Anchorite like room, is an
Anthill being suckled,
By the Beheaded caterpillar, of

A Metallic volcano, &

              Yellow!!! Dancing
                    Cows, welcoming

An,   early,
          Appalachin   SPRING?

The Apotheosis of Salvador Dali

It mighta been around the era of
The Rob Ford Scandal,
Or maybe even Before then,
That I experienced the "cosmogonic" Realization
That when Salvador Domingo Felipe Jacinto Dali
i Domènech
 Died,
He became, (or RE-became)
Our Supreme Ruling deity which
Explains why Our world,
IS,
The way it now, IS, (or has always, been)
& My Zealot-like, faith, in this Belief, is absolutely Un
-shakeable!! Just ask my friends.
I see His genetic finger Prints
& Fluid,
Precise Brush strokes everywhere I, turn!
Turn,
Everywhere I Look, I see his Nuclear
Logic, His Microphotographic brush strokes, His
Hallucinogenic
Humour,
Reigning SUPREME …. I hear him
Laugh when I
Open a Newspaper on the Subway,
& read something like " Hot Sauce Mom found
        guilty,
of giving her children,
A SPICY PUNISHMENT", or "More than 250 people worldwide have

Died while taking selfies in the last six years"
I see…… him, When I flick on, someone else's flat screen
Tv, & hear about
Some Vampiric Dictator, using the Drained productive citizens of
his Once, Prosperous, resource rich Country
As a MASSIVE, human Shield!
I see him in the unvarnished! Strobo
-scopic portrait of a Polymorphous
Pervert, PULVERIZED, by a
Hot, female
Teacher, punching one of her 1st Grade students in the
Mouth!!!
& an En-ameled, Auric egg, containing a
                    Black!
Misshapen Pearl cast daily before the, crudest, Most
Succulent of, Swine! Even in the Ravishing
 Draped recumbent figure of, a Taxidermied
Polar Bear covered with a
Charred! Fleshless gnawed skeleton of Flawless, Jewels,
& a Blue swan, Filled, with Pomegranates
& Explosives he is
SEEN,
He is seen in a Fresh,
Virginal form, CLAMOR
      -ing
For expression, jump kick, ing its way out
of the Moist! Womb of the great,
Daringly dressed mother waving a false
Flag of liquid stone, emblazoned
With the image of a silver, un
-splinterable spear that heals every single wound,
it EVER caused!
In Every "Black Pete" celebration in Amsterdam
& brave, testicle-less soldiers sacrificing their lives
for the interests of corporations that don't give a fuck about them,
& even less of a shit about their Families
He is- seen,
In the hilarity of the death of …David Carradine,

He is Seen, He is seen
In the person of Caitlyn/Bruce Jenner & The Now
Revealed secret lives of the once squeaky clean Michael
Jackson & Bill Cosby
He is Seen in the Vegetative growths, SPROUTing from
The closed mouths of
Beautiful women suffering from SEVERE, Male,
pattern Baldness he is Seen!
In Photosynthesis, algorithms, "Tentacle
Porn", Metatron's cube, pregnant, infants & Osmosis He is ....
Seen! Is he
Not?
He is Seen in all Our history Books!
I see him in Quantum physics! I
See Him in the Vermeerian, curtain, which is actually
The Invisible, Hidden!
Monumental face of the Dionysiac frenzy of the Glittering
Scales of a
Flying, 3 spined fish!
I see him in the actions of The Sacred, sobbing! Un
-seen doctor in Stockholm Sweden drugging her thugged
Out male, patients with milk chocolate covered
Strawberries LACED, with
"Rohypnol",
& Locking them in her sound proof, pleasure ...... Chamber,
He is, Seen!!!
In how we treat the Planet, In how we treat, Animals, each other,
& "Etc" .....He is Seen,
In City planners paying Lip service, to the ideas of Jane Jacobs, while canon-
izing
Her, a Saint,
But doing the Exact opposite of what she Cassandra'd! He Is
Seen,
I see His draughtsmanship, I see his "Paranoiac Critical Method",
I See his Genetic finger prints Everywhere!
I turn, TURN,
Everywhere I look, Look! I see his phantasmagoric Logic,
Reigning SUPREME, Like I told you,

…The Whole 2016 Election, was PURE him,
The Inquisition,
The Crusades,
The Dancing manias, Minstrel shows,
Witch hunts,
& The results of the French, & Russian Revolutions
Were Pure DALINIAN,
Were they not?
Indigenous cultures of the World generously rolling
out the Red carpet to the greedy, Unscrupulous
Bastards that ALMOST Smuggled their "actual" Doom, was
PURE Dali, was it
Not?
Like when you hear someone objectifying or Stereotyping themselves, & then
Bitching about how they are being
STEREO TYPED or OBJECTIFIED,
I can't help but laugh, the fact that he is Our Supreme Ruling
                Deity,
Has given me back my sense of humour about the Workings of,
This World,
When I see the right arm & bare breasts of an "enigmatic, High
Stepping" girl with a collaged, Gaudily
Colored head of a ….. parrot,
I can't help now, but, Giggle… I can't help now, but Dance, though
I am cursed! with two Left,
feet,
made out of- Clay.
…… The Full moonlight prostrates itself at "The Selection
Of Erotic vignettes" of
Horny! Rubenesque ex-wives giving into
"Temptation" for me
at the Blue, "Cannibalistic Apples" of
His Severed,
Unwinged Feet like a Rabid! Obedient Hound, Or
a HEROIC young, Spit fire Wearing only, a long black t-shirt,
With Bright!
Refrigerator White letters that

Spell.........."Go Fuck Yourself", as she insufflates a line of
"Ketamine" in a
Stall of the crowded Mens washroom
At the Cineplex theatre,
At
Yonge & Eglington, before she sits, down
To Re-watch ... "La La Land" With.......
"Me"☺
While I close my Eyes & see an InFURiated, Miniature, Sex reversed
Mustang galloping, triumphantly. out of the Pink!, Etio
-lated,
Shark infested
......Sea,
In the White Shadow, of The Blue gardenia, of "The Petrified
Forest",
In the White shadow, of the last Astronaut to ever, walk!
Upon the Bright, side, of the
-Moon.....
No Burning giraffe, Ladies & Gentleman, no other Avatar, guru, or Deity,
Can obscure Salvador Dali from
Our view, Now,
His very name, Salvador, Means "Saviour", He
Is Now the giver of life, & the source of All
That is, was! & will ....Ever
Be.

"Blessed is
He"
"Blessed is He, Our Lord," Our
God,
Creator of the holographic multiverse, Salvador Dali,
Salvador Dali!
(Sheathed in **Astrakhan**)
Is now he whom the, Tetrachs fear, & Pray to
As their overdue demise, comes near, Salvador Dali! Is
Now he whom, the Universal laws exist, Only as,
Playthings,
Salvador Domingo Felipe Jacinto

Dali i Domènech,
Is now he, whom, separates the Wheat, from the Straw,
& the Thick! From the …..Thin,

…..With Gala as His Female aspect,
With Gaudi as His architect,
& Garcia Lorca, St. John of the Cross,
& St. Gregory Corso, THE DIVINE,
as His messengers,
With Wagner as his musical director,
& …..Us, Yes,…….
"Us",
As His Unruly, Halfwitted! Slowly awakening Children,
Long!
Loooooooooooonnnnnngggggggggggggg
-gggggg
-g

Long May he REIGN,

Amen.

"The Script for Taxi Driver scared the shit out of Everybody"

Study! Revolt! Struggle..... Success!?

We shed our ineffable raiments of
Tormented flesh....
& Queen street west Morphed into a Ballet
At Rush hour as
Badly aging pop stars
Declaring the ACTUAL Divinity,
Of the "Fair limbed harpies"
Genius enough to
Dig ME, were
Being haunted by the In
-satiable ghosts! Of Groupies
Past.
During the desperate, "Retributive hour".

In which I Magus'd your
Sceptered Beast!

A few years ago We sprinted, I SPED blindly into
The belly of "IT", of
Whom you are still crawling out!
I know THE SHIVERING NARCISSUS of a yellow afternoon,
Wielding the parched Dagger! Of Mummi
-fied WIN
 ter under the Deflatable SUN unrisen-

I've best friend-ed the Brooding jubilant Animals Punc
-tured longing managing their
Feeble perceptions
Ascending the white skies, with Rolling, MERGING,
Black clouds like "Enoch",
Upon a fiery, barbed! Stained glass
Steed!

I'm sorry My fellow tribesmen who have
Gifted Me more
Than I ever thought I could
NEED...........I'm
Adventuring Home empty handed from the

HUNT.

I learned "the Mysteries of the Red Gold" under
The untamed tutelage, of the
ComPANion of
Nymphs?

I know a Burnt child afeared of the long extinguished
Fires flame.

I've Learned Study! Revolt! Struggle! .....Success?

....We shed Our ineffable raiments
Of tormented flesh,   on the Night of a
BLUE moon.

& Nakedly we ROAM, the star Domed

Light!

...... " Vulnerable to

E
V
E
R
Y
  T
    H
      I
        N
          G"

Travis Bickle Goes to Hollywood (Variations on the opening lines of Dante's "Inferno")

      "Midway
upon the Journey of My Life" I strayed
off of the Straight path &
Woke to find myself in the guise
Of a ritually Maimed
        mustang
 Losing the fruitless race, against time in
The dark woods, alone, grasping,
      Stretching
For that vague, Legendary, un-onion skinned light, like A
 "Brash young cowboy" attempting
          to
Pick up a pale! Visibly hung, over
Waitress wearing overly expensive,
      shoes, Too
Tight! For comfort, on a midwinter
Night....
Too HUMID To ….. Bear,

      Midway
Through, Our Odyssey of, Life,
I found myself Needing an Increasing amount of
(Paste your favorite Inebriants "Here") just
     to be
Able to stomach, the dawning day.
I Found myself, there, sacrificed on the
      Bright!

Neronian hearthstone like an Innocent!
Sleek!
Insolent Dove smouldering crystal
SMOOTH at noon, day,
In a Dark, Liminal forest because
The straight forward gateway, had been
Closed, irrevocably to,
Me,
I found myself walking up Yonge street, alone, wondering
what
Would happen if Travis Bickle went to Hollywood, Washington,
& Ottawa as
Summer coagulated, Into Autumn
I,
I Found myself with a sweet, peg leg, Captaining your
Magnificent! Upholstered, Hole filled ship of Heavy,
Stone, alone, like I said,
Adrift! The Molten sea, Where even the broad Daylight,
Seemed,   "Harsh".

Midway
Through my Pilgrimage of Life
I,
Discovered that all of the Movie Palaces &
Graveyards, We used to, Slink to
For refuge in Our, Teens, have
Recently been, Demolished, &, Converted
into
Tiny!! Over priced
Condos,
& "Saks Fifth Avenue"s ….. With valet Parking
like
An Adroit! Shifter of …. Indistinct Shape, Carved
In Soft Granite…….. 6 Meters
-High,
Leaping over toppled, Deciduous, Simian
Haunted Trees,
& a silver Haired Model Sprawling in the

54

arms
of an Organism, of humble beginnings
Growing,
Sprouting into a BLOATED, extravagant Monster
Of ......Technology, & "The Piper at the Gates of
          Dawn",
Witnessing the Gargoyles of Materialism & The
Ogresses of "Transience", unveil their inner
Beauty, to the Visionary offspring of the fated union,
        of
Cassandra, &, **Tiresias,** While Raw Footage of fleeing, Terrified
People cowering in,
Horror! At
The Largest mass shooting, & Natural
Disaster, in every sunken Continents,
Scarcely known history, Is Looped, continuously....on My Parents
-Tv.

       I
found myself in a Liminal forest Dark & saw a
Ladder of Polished bones, Rising
In the sky, I saw "The hideous pink décor"
of the contemporary vice dens on the Barbary coast!
& The 6 corners of the gnarled lemon of
      -the MOON, I saw
The Solidification of every Shadow! I witnessed The
Dissolution of, My ..... "I", & a Tender, memorial,
on a desolate   pier,
I wandered, veered off the oft beaten Path,
& saw
Exorbitant, Unimaginable delights! Grim! Unsettling sights,
FORTUITOUS GIFTS atop the scrap
      heap,
"a Big gleaming Machine", all the treasures of Arabia,
& saw Howlin Wolf gigging for a fish sandwhich,.. only.
& the Gnawed! Chewed, licked skull, of a poached Albino
    Pygmy Elephant!
My little Eye spied The puzzling toleration

Of VAST inequities,
    I saw
The Harrowing prognosis & the Stark assessment
    Of a Sharp!
Uplifted axe, held by a Living, man!
Rematerializing in our land, of RIVET-ing
Ghosts, as
The Crackling, Emerald fire was Squirming, Streaking
Across that country of ..... Wine .... It's Thick heavy -Smoke,
& "Screeching Synths",   Inundating
the, Firmament......

    Midway
In My Battle through This particular Existence
I lost sight of Ariadne's Golden Thread leading
    Me safely through the Labyrinth &
Forgot the higher! Wisdom hard WON, & Found
Myself loathing MYSELF, My species, My
City, My Vocation! My Avocation, & loathing

    ® Senescence ©

The World, & even –You,
Dear reader,
For the straight forward path seemed lost to
Me,
I found myself suffering A strange, near
Debilitating Affliction of the Spirit,
& Google-ing, almost Daily,
    "The
Least painful ways to Die", (insert the name of
Any random porn site HERE)
Esoteric Exposal, "the Lonely Vagabond" Katie Longboat
&, Anton Newcombe on "Twitter", & ....So
on,

I found myself Hanging around the U of T Campus in an
Earnest go at Befriending the young Chemist(s)

who will
Stumble upon the Psychedelic Dissociative(s)
Of the Future.... Until, Inevitably, I would undergo
An Abrupt! Seismic, Teutonic shift, of Perspective &, was able to cackle,
      "Chortle"
Again, at Myself, Our World, & ......it
ALL,
I found myself remembering, that this Life is
Just a- cruel, cruel & beautiful chapter
In an Eternal story, & a school, a Temple, an antechamber
of Initiation..... For
        the soul,
& Every day that Dawns, upon

    " us",

is supposedly A gift in the, Dark wood,
As The Creator! Preserver &, Destroyer become
      - ONE-

"Midway, through! Our Journey, of-
      Life"

Infant Monkeys eating Aspartame/
"CODY JARRETT"

On Tranquilizers
Your astral body shoots up out of the Soil as
   A blade of grass in a vast garden
Prompting Me to shout! "You are the
        EARTH"!

& You ARE! .... Aren't we ALL?
Your rare baby Blue! Armoured,   tank of a body
Becomes an Immense ocean
Full of captainless, ships........
   Conspicuous pick pockets
        Drinking,
   Calculated, Water!!
A
Person in the la-ter stages of Alzheimers
Rediscovering their forgotten lives
      Via   photo, Poli-
Police provocateurs are LACED
Throughout the peaceful protests
where
The computer generated image, of a
Young Marlon Brando is Randomly gifting
A Thousand cheap, thrills
      Consummating
In a RAW,   Instant- A FLOWER-
             As
People of all races & creeds fly

Across
The triangular canvas of the, star wealthy,
Sky!
So- So why!! Terrorist cells of proud parents
Surveilling
An Organization, of babies making

Snow angels in the
Shifting,
Garbage littered
Sand??

….No lifeguard is on duty, Ladies & Gentlemen, No
Sunsets & NO sadness born
of Joyous Eve
-nings are
Teasing lucky ARCS of
Visual LIGHT! No

Hidden owls crystal Eagle! No

Embarking upon the soundless foam cock
-pits moaning pilots Stately!
Disembodied voice of LIQUID, speckled,
Philosophic - stone? Ari
-sing from out of the tender,
Seal skin boats!
Of our cold grey sailors inces
-tous mother AWED,
By our one color Painting! At
The "Epicenter" of the EDGE- The Dead,
 Coarse, peasants the Dead, coarse
Peasants Rebel Chinese along The
River, Laborers,…. millions- Only-
 Only the Vampires escaped "Black country
Rock"
Unscathed.

"The- "The Tigers are disappearing from the
Sleepwalking, Chain sawed forests!" They
say,

"The Famished tigers are disappearing from the
Sleepwalking, chain sawed Forests!"
Their Oysters have been –DRAINED!

& the Beached Dolphins & whales Alas, are on their
way To Brunch!
     . A Brown,
 Miniature! Sex
reversed
Under nourished Mustang, is
Galloping (Triumphantly) out Of the Pink, Etio
-lated Grey Swan Infested   –Sea– It's time to, Do-
It's time to do what loyal followers do when
They find out their beloved leader is "Wrong"?
It's time for armies to French kiss   French
Kiss French Kiss Foam, flung! From
 a   Deep ships voice!

New, KINGDOMS!! For haggard pariahs to, seek!
New Ways to manipulate public Opinion,
To accept the agendas of the
"Ruling Classes! " … Fresh Symbols,
NEW WAYS TO BURN OUT! New, Raptures!
To defileth thine body drifting toxic clouds
          Of volcanic, ash!

The sound of the Lone loon singing
Instant "Gratification"-

The sound of the Lone Loon   singing
Instant gratification, across
The fake, Lake?
Competitive food eating contests being
     Held in this, World, Where,

Billions are STARV,

              ing,!   Revel,

       BACCHANALI

-AN!!

      .....Mock - Funeral....

When Harry doesn't get his Laundry

It's raining people holding umbrellas outside
In my multiple summers of drought!
"Hasta la Victoria Siempre",
"Hasta la Victoria Siempre",
"HASTA LA VICTORIA SIEMPRE"!
Which when translated into English means
"Keep fighting until Victory, always" or "Forever, until Victory"
Don't let the balloons fly away,
Ladies, who used to be elegant sirs
Of the Bastille jury,
FARMERS OF THE OCEAN!!
I know no notion, no Thelemic witch
Concocted potion that can help you
Answer thee essential questions
"Where did we come from"? "Why are we here"?
"What is Life"? "What is reality"? "What is
NORMAL"?
"Who created God"?
"Where does all of the shit we recycle
Off of our computers go"?
& "Uncle, what ails thee"?
I've given up! Trying to figure them out myself!
I don't want to know,
Scorched Earth! Frozen sea? Smashing
Glassy water!!

3 large planets are orbiting a dwarf star!
The closets are ajar, & so are the doors?
The media created monsters are on the loose!

-the baby molar tooth,
Of a recently discovered Hominid,
The little white fragment of a hand bone,
Sickened by the slaughter!?
A wealth of onions,
Brings a poverty of dry tears to my electric eyes,
I close those eclectic eyes in the void, & I see
A smelly sound,
I close those kohl accented eyes, & I see Blue?!
I look at Jay + Sarah 98= Forever,
Scrawled unto THIS bus shelter,
On this rainy day, & I wonder
If the mysterious couple who wrote it
Are still together somewhere,
Transcending the 5 elements,
Mining the turquoise,
Raising the Non-existent children,
Of an OVER party!
Plotting to do the various things
That make grown men cry!!
I attempt, I TRY to gaze at everything
In an ecstatic state of complete reverence,
There are Spies, Mosquitos, Hyenas, Tipsters, & Flies,
Everywhere around us?
False comraderie, & a billion invisible frequencies
Surround us!
"Everything is a double edged sword"!
Everything in existence is a wonderful work of art!
Created by someone,
But I genuinely can't fathom who!
Nor can anyone else, really,
-Somewhere a scythe is being sharpened!
SomeWHERE someONE is sporting your
Thick Christmas sweater on a summer beach
Sounding the tocsin,
While everyone is listening to the silence!
NON VIOLENCE erupts in the fossilized forests,
Where childrens imaginary friends

Go to DIE!
Black smoke billowing from the depths of
Your cluster bombed buildings!
Polluting my extravagant sky!
Your hoary hands are now in somebody ELSE'S
Empty pockets,
My wallets' still un-moneyed!
It can't En-salmon anyone ELSE'S,
Shallow sea?
The steps are Steep, the Presidents teleprompter
Is messing up! The I-phones & Blackberrys
Are mercifully melting in the fire,
I've seen what's under the kilt!
I'VE SEEN WHAT'S UNDER THE KILT!
The fruit of the people's sweat & toil
Is being squandered!
I WAS BORN IN A GRAVEYARD!! & I'm
Going to get buried in your hospital?
Celebrities are their new deities!
"All order has been vanquished",
All the rules have been previously broken, Hecate,
Can you think of anything else
Left for us to break?
Our colony of cats! Is going to the
 DOGS!
Anubis is beckoning us to follow his lead.
O! The carnage!
O! The excitement of the way of Blended extremes-
The now barren in our incomprehensible lives
Shall one day become Prosperous,
Insert any country's name
Here's War planes shower me & my anti-heroic people
With WHITE PHOSPHOR...OUS!!
& now I smell like.....Chinatown,
When
Harry doesn't get his, Laundry.

Gargling with Bleach

It was like glancing up from the
Obituary column, with horror, & fascination,
& catching a sneak peek of a fabulous, vocal-less opera? Or!
.... Hitler,
Facing Rasputin, in a
Staring contest, from Behind a barred window....

The Landslide swept through an Alaskan, town,
& a toxic yellow cloud hovered over,
Sudbury,
As a Rhodes scholar was caught surfing, on
The roof of a pickup truck......Speeding
On the highway...... &

Baseball sized hail, fell from the sky.

It was like, glancing up from the
Obituary column, I remember quite clearly, "Twas
On a foggy night", just like, tonight, in fact,
Was it NOT, Dear
Heart?
It was like, Gargling with, Bleach?
& catching a sneak peek behind the mock,
Tragic farce,

 A
"Reposing Sphinx", & A
"Captured Harlequin", jumped
Off of the mosaic floor, of a

"Cold Dead Garden", A
Man raised in a geometrical prison, was forced, alone,
Into
The Amazonian rainforest, as
A Black sun, set,
Over the Pink, etiolated
Sea.....

It was like looking up from surveying
The utter Devastation, with self-inflicted, horror,
& disinterested, FASCINATION, the
Doomed crew pleaded with the pilot of the plane to turn, around,
Before the Crash...

We
Watched the blue moon Rise over the city,
From Your 9th storey balcony, that I
Am too afraid to stand on, "Sometimes", due, to my wari
-ness of..... Heights.

A Toronto party goer, made his abrupt, transition,
Into the great "Here after".....After
Snorting,
What he believed to be, a
Generous,
Delicious line of "K"!
 but was,
The coroner revealed, today, the lethal Drug,
"Fentanyl"?

It was like seeing a seeress convert poison into
Your favourite wine, and contaminated water,
Into champagne,
It was like putting down a RIVETING,
Well told story, (So I've been told), or "the passage of time, into

Eternity", or,
Eternity into,   Time-

It was like glancing up from the
Obituary column,
& groping a sneak, peek, of a,
Vocal-less,
Mind expanding, opera… from
Behind a barred, window, or….Hitler! Facing
RASPUTIN, in a staring
Contest?

5 Shaded, Black Circles for Madama Butterfly

1.

Madama Butterfly once left my mid-90's Cellphone In HIS,
Coke
Dealers
Car.

'Twas
Her "Flaws" that Cupid'd, MEEEE
-EE,

& We didn't even know, them,

.....YET......

2.

"Citizens of My Country, behold
Me,
I start out on my Last journey. I look for
The last time at the light of the Sun.
The God of Hades will take me alive,
I shall not have known marriage,
No wedding song will have echoed
My Name,
Death,
Will Espouse Me", From

Jean Cocteau's version of Sophocles's
"Antigone".

& "Im Not looking for ANYONE, to
Save, me,
I Just need somebody to Hold My soft,
Skeletal Hand,
As I tip toe around the Hungry MOUTH,
Of My, Open......Grave...."
Which is From an old poem By
.... ME.

& as You can clearly, See,
The Perfect QUOTE,
Was always sitting upon the Illustrious
METAL,

Of Her chapped ... Lips.

3.

Thelonious Monk had a picture of Billie Holiday,
TACKED, on to the Ceiling of His
Room,

& Me? I hava picture of HER,
Taped,
onta MINE.

4.

A Terminally Ill teenager receiving an
Early Christmas, In
Mid June,
"The Fall of Icarus" By Rodin, A

Bottomless bag made from the skin of a mythical Crane
With the Delicately woven face,
Of Medusa,
A Doctor, in Stockholm Sweden, drugging her
Thugged out male patient with Milk Chocolate
Covered Strawberries LACED, With
"Rohypnol",
An Albino Pygmy elephant Doggie Padlin'
In the Indian Ocean,
Rolled up Dollar Bills, Bills!
Powder Smeared Cd cases, & Tables,
Nude Women Spooning our Fully Clothed Companion, Excru-CIATing
Bliss,
Poignant- Invasion!!
…A Bitter Truth CLOAKED, in a tasteless
Joke,
The Prefiguration of an exhausting, Cinematic montage of a
Mysterious Creature attempting to get "Sober",
Amidst the controversial delusion of our CONSTANT,
Party,
An Electronic pitch shifting device,
An old portable Synthesizer with a joystick,
That fits inside a suitcase,
& a Dirty, dissonant, left handed
Guitar,
"Strange Circular Flying Shapes"
& the Turquiose Mask, of a
Feathered
Snake,
The Yellow rose of …Texas, & The Purple, one,
Of Cairo,
The remains of Jimmy Hoffa,
Amelia Earheart,
Rocco Perri,
The count of St.Germain,
Fulcanelli, Frank Matthews
&, D.B Cooper,

"The Fearlessness that comes from having nothing
to Lose",
& Thousands of Killer bees cryogenically frozen in their Hives-An
Altar constructed of Horns Mounted on, a
Crescent Moon,
…New Years eve, Christmas! Hanukkah!
Ramadan,
Halloween, Easter, "The Geopolitical Child watching the Birth Of the New
Man", "The treasure of the Sierra Madre"
& Your, birthday,
All sewn Into one composite Monster,
"A shocking,, much needed departure from
The USUAL Formulas",
& The Broomstick of the wicked Witch of
The
WEST!!!!

Madama Butterfly Possess'd, it, ALLLLLL
LLLLL
Lllllllllllllllllllll
-llllll
-l.

Some…… Place…..

5.

Her face, was the one thing
I longed to see at the close
Of each
Day
….. When my old life got 360'd
on me,
& the money & party supplies
Vanished,
& my fake friends all, spl-it,

Her two, wish fulfilling!
Blood stained
  Hands,
Were the only
Ones,
That offered, me,
The stark white
Light!
  Of
The midnight
- sun.

Madama Butterfly,

Madama
  B!
Gift'd me THAT,
Which
This world of "Ours",
Could
  -n
    't…..

&-& she tucked (before she
Departed)
In my picked,
Pock
  -et

"The
Ultimate
Boon"?

Olga

Beau-
B-
Beautiful,
Crim-
Beautiful,
Criminally Un-venera-
Beautiful,
Criminally un-venerated Girl who currently works
At "Dollarama"!!

Sovereign Queen, of ALL,
That doesn't yet....
Exist,

When You saw me Examining you as if You were
"The 3rd
Brightest star in the constellation of Aquarius"
& didn't Cringe,
or shudder, at the recognition of My photosyn, thetic,
Consolatory
Gaze,
but brazenly interlocked with, mine, a prurient one of
your own,
while sporting an
ear to ear-
          smile,,
I thought not, not of a
Slowly gestating Fetus's cartilage HARDEN-ing

into bone, or a homosexual gangster rapper licking
     VAGINAS,
That have red wine stained
Teeth,
& "The Great despoilment" at Hand, Sweet
     girl,
When you looked at
Me,
Like a refugee in the brutal cold, in urgent need of, winter
...... clothes,

or A Transgender
         boy,
Forced to wrestle... girls, I for
-got,
  about Our " Grim Predicament", & the supposed
"Dark age ahead",
Instead! An extended glimpse of a
     Bright!
Wooden! Quixotic,
Space,
 & ocean going Steamboat, sailing towards
The FRESH vist
-as,
& The ICE gleaming Pinnacles
of Our golden, platinum
plated
Future! Is what I, seen,
I Fell for ....you,
Like a Kamikaze pilot, in world war..... 2,
I felt,
A record shattering warmth! & something,
I cannot quite name, In your
Self effaced presence, I Felt!
     I felt
Around my Scrawny, neck "The Black silk, noose", that,
......Failed.....

Beaut-
B-
Beautiful, un- Beautiful Under
       -rate-
Beautiful under rated girl I have never actually talked to,
& Probably never ....will,
When You Clasped my skeletal, Well lotioned
Hand that afternoon,
You restored my eviscerated faith, in our
Troubled,
Schizophrenic Species, Sad, isn't
                it,
That it was that, easy, no? When You,

Gazed into my eyes like a keen
Young, Scientist, for soooooo longgggg
-g,
I almost felt .... uncomfortable,
          & had
To avert, them, As someone in line, began .... clearing their
.....Throat.....

...... Beautiful,
Criminally Un-venerated girl,
Intimidating, Equal of, any,
Celebrated
Beauty, of OUR Time, & anyyyyyy
other, When
You noticed me looking at
You like an Archeologist, unearthing a Startling
New -Fossil,
& didn't cringe at the sight of
...... Me,
like the rest of them
     −do,
I Knew, that for
you,

I could successfully beat a few
Kenyans,
& .... Ethiopians, In
 a long distance -marathon......

In your bleak, times of trouble, &
the uncertain Years to,
Come,
My two, skeletal, well lotioned
     hands,
Could be the ones,
That free your famished tiger, from its
Bird..... cage,
& Hoist in
Your Wayward
direction, the stark, White –
un-onion skinning light,

   of ....

The Black, lactating
   Sun.

The Zodiacal Year of the metal Rat

The Global Pandemic hit, just as I
                 Was nearing the tail end of my
                 Prison sentence,
                 I had recently been shuffled to
                 A Minimum security facility, &
Was studying Alchemy, Scarcely recorded History, &
                 The work of John Keely, & Hermann
                 Von Helmholtz,
                 & My Wife & Kids could come
                 Spend weekends with
                 Me, ALAS,
But then "It"   happened…

                 I had just started My dream
Job & booked my 1st, long awaited
Trip outside the confines
Of My Native land,
My first Full Length volume
Of Poetry was accepted by
A Publisher, & was slated to be
                 Released within the year,
I had two tickets apiece,
To see both of my favourite
Bands live, in concert…
Finally!
But then The Global Pandemic –Struck.…

After the conflagration of a decade & a little more of being broke,
Sleeping on Couches, Floors, & 3 computer
       Chairs put together somewhere
       In "The Outer Limits", of
       "The Twilight Zone",
       I had found a solid connection
       For (substance name Censored),
       & had a place to call * Home *
       with someone who loved me,
       & to whom I was engaged,
       I had cut down on my Drinking,
       & Began hitting the Gym,
       As we were going
       To get Married,
       In May,
But then the Global Pandemic HIT, in the
Chinese Year of the Metal Rat,
 & now we're both quarantine-ing at our Place
Looking out the smudged up windows
at an empty street of anxiety on a Friday night
       Downtown with
       Only a few people scurrying
       Around to eke out a living,
       & wrassle up Groceries & Booze,
       wearing surgical masks,
Wondering if Our already troubled, schizophrenic
       World is going to get even
       Creepi
       -errrrrrrrrrrrrrrrrrrrrrrrrr
rrrrrrrrrrrrrrrrrrrrrrrrrrrrrrrrr
     rrrrrr...

       I had just recovered from Minor
Surgery, & a heavy bout
Of the Flu,
Which really slid everything into
Perspective for me,
& I was ready to boldly, surgically attack life

Exuberantly,
With a Razor sharp knife,
& not take anything, for granted,
I knew exactly what I had to do,
To get where I needed to be in Life,
& was ready, truly ready,
Frothing, champing
at the bit, to walk, my big poetic
Alms giving talk, & mend the frayed ties
With those who I felt had did me
Wrong, in the past,
& count my abundant blessings, & revel,
Dance! FROLIC,
Within the Archons' Creation,
                I had actually reached a
Period in Life where I was balanced,
Excited, & Genuinely, Optimistic,
& "Happy""
& Then,
        The Global Pandemic HIT, ... In
The Zodiacal Year, of the
                Metallic
                    Rat

Sky Masterson

1.

Hideous Basements!
Infected by light-
"KITTENS TERRIFIED OF CARPET"-
Puking up dry water in a diamond
Hell!
Serpents of the Universe who's un-
Hatched eggs are planets!
Eagle headed
Goddesses slowly pecking your
Ways out of My cosmic egg?
The emaciated cows of India are skinny dipping in?
The Emaciated cows of India sniffing
Something
That probed my brain are skinny dipping into
Our sparsely wooded area to the grating sound of "Spare change",
"SPARE CHANGE"! "Spare ---change"?
Our rich bastards are HEAVING themselves poorly
Out of the stained glass windows Windows windows,
Windows of the sky
Scrapers & OVER priced condos that
Tower over us Godzilla-ly!
Like "MOTHRA",
...a 13ᵗʰ century woodcut of a dazzling asteroid
Sand paints a white streak, across the
Board straight aristocratic back
Of a regal black sun as a
Newly minted meteor

Shaves the soft stubble off of
The planets Earths face!
Our full chaordic stomachs are GROWLING
In unison inside the tree house of "The Teahouse of
The August Moon"!

BrEaKiNg NeWS!!!??!
"Rauschenberg has erased De Kooning",
People are standing in front of
Churches, mosques, synagogues,
Ashrams, & Temples!
Burning the Torah, the Talmud, The Qu'ran,
The Book of Mormon, Dianetics,
& every kind of sutra, treatise, & Bible!
To ignite a combustible crowd!
Surprise storms have left 242 dead, knocked out power
To millions of homes on the east coast of
The United States,
War planes are thundering over Libya! Afghanistan, Syria, & Iraq!
STILL!
An extreme heat wave hath claimed 10 lives
In Quebec today-
Thousands of Israelis are taking to the streets to
Protest the rising costs of Living-
Lindsay Loh-
Lindsay Lohan is back in Rehab today! "The way
You sleep, can Reduce
 Wrinkles"?
A pearl faced dolphin who may or may not
Sleep talk in BEACHED WHALE song
Is jumping aboard an aerial boat
Today, injuring
A woman in South Florida, Tomorrow,
A Number of Erotic suspects Euthanized
On the Gaza strip of the Meth lab, of our
Collective imagination,
Tsunamis of Unsettling sensations!!
BLOATED, water logged bodies, FLASH floods!

Rolling blackouts!
Deserted pets, separated families!
Evacuated cities full of centaurs being ENVELOPED
in rising walls of worst fears
GENEROUSLY erected,
3 Alpha males are sipping king cans of liquid genitals
In Trinity Bell woods park as we
speak!
O, Battered Runaways!! LO! Elegant Technological savages
Becoming "Loose" & ... "Scary"!
Your Abusive! Alcoholic father, is
Entering
The Realm of the Mothers?
Abraxas =365!
"Seat belts & smoke Detectors save lives"!
"According to the Franklin Parish Sheriff's
Office, Sharmeka Moffit was wearing a Kanye west
T-shirt when the assailants allegedly doused her
With racial slurs, & gasoline, & scrawled the letters
"NAACP" upon the hood of her beat up truck",
A Bullied B.C teens' suicide has sparked political action in Ottawa,
& a Rescued dog shot in the head 50 times by a pellet gun
In Nova Scotia,
Has found a loving new Home....

Must the resplendent contents,
Of my petrified bowls BEWARE
Your raging spoon? & "the ides of March"!
WHO WILL BE OUR TRUSTED COMPANIONS,
In our final moments,
Within THIS physical plane?
I'm CHANGING the, channel....

I'm
TURNING
Off
The news
NOW.

I'm loitering on the marble STREETS of
"Oblivion",

Awaiting
THE dawn.....

2.

"For I say unto Liberating oppressors,
There are 2 ways to conquer, & enslave
My nation,
One is by the sword,
& the other is by Debt",
"For I say unto you it would
Be easier for a camel to pass through
The eye of a needle
Then for a rich man to enter
The kingdom of Heaven",
"The Rose has long been the flower of love,
Its beauty & its thorns remind us
Of the mixed blessing we receive
When we open ourselves to love"
"James Dean offered American audiences,
A new image of the rebel as
Poetic anti-hero as the misunderstood
But vulnerable herald of a new generation,
The boy in anguish as a disturbed, animal,
So in need of love, that nothing else
Has any reality",
"In one hand, I offer them something
Like Brando saying Fuck you,
& I have Clift in the other one saying
Please help me",
My Ultraviolent, Cesare Borgia like pen,
Is recklessly wielding other people's quotes
But ay!
"Alice Bailey criticized national groups
Based on what she believed were their

Violations of the spirit of Unity
& Brotherhood,
She believed that an individuals
Primary allegiance is to humanity,
& not to any sub group within it",
I'll save that shit for another day!
-a million superficial differences divide "US",
There is no such thing as being "Civilized"!
& "Nothing is solid",
We emerge out of the bright darkness
Into the view of Samyaza singing the songs
That were once composed in honor of pagan
   GODS!
    LIMP DEMAND!!!
Divine abominations standing strong
With weak erection,
Shouting "Love has to be re-invented" like Rimbaud
Recommended,
"Life MUST be changed"!
A whole generation of kids cursed by narrowed consciousness
Are being exposed to things
Their dipsomaniacal parents spoon feeding
Said children to Moloch!
The government Blob! & THE BORG will never know!
Circles & sheets of sound, Musical noise!
GIRLS GONE wild, elderly women going MAD!!
War pigs getting awarded our Nobel peace prize!
Banksters
Head scratchingly named "TIME" magazines
"Person of the year"!
Thousand year old prophecies of mass
Destruction,
Or Global awakening!!
Alien or Deity intervention or
.......NOTHING....
The ending of an aeon, & the beginning of another,
Even the priestess Pythia,
The Oracle of Apollo at DELPHI & my old friend

Susan Munro,
Don't know what's going to happen,
......What a STRANGE, & exciting
      TIME, to be
        STUCK!!!

In Existence.

For Lana Shields

The Swan drawn Chariots of my, Conspicuously, Dressed,
Fugitive! Is Clasped, Asphixiatingly, Within
Your Invisible, Initiatory- Hands, as
The Damp footprints soft, imprint, Eva
-porates,
from the surface, of the shifting,…..Garbage littered
- Sand,
The IMMENSE solitude of My self exile is HAUNTED,   by Your
–Image,
& Your distant embrace, is
The only remaining portal,
To the realm, to
which I constantly pine…. To,
Return,-
I see You Gallivant! I watch you
Dawdle, meander, CAVORT around the Downtown streets, awash
In NEON, like a Gentle!   NON
---- Violent,
Even More Alienated, rendition,
of
Travis Bickle, in consensual- Reality, But
In my fertile, unshackled Imagination We laze about, in your Recently
Discovered, Tomb, like a
Drowning man BEACHED, by a
female Lifeguard, &The Decree, of the Cats paw-of
-Fate, Listening, Listen
-ing
 to that Elusive Tune, the cicadas Croon, Outside a Scottish village
that b(h)ops, into -"being ", Once!! Every OTHER …..Century,

Few
people are supposedly drawn to a Solitary, Organism, whom Others
Avoid, ridicule! ...... Neglect,-
 Rejects!
 & Shun, but I
.... Am. most people, are criminally blind, to, your peculiar
Magnificence, but I'm
... Not.
Few men can sincerely Love! The under Loved! Women, Whom
Others hardly, ever -notice,
 But I,
Do.
& I don't even REALLY, know,
You!!   I!   Know
a HeighTEN-ed, FLAW
        -less,
 Larger than "Mortal", you! Or a Crude, Distorted! **Facsimile,**
of ......You,
 I,
Know a better! (or worse) ...You!! That
  may only exist inside my, mind, that I Double! Triple
Project upon the silver screen, of the REAL...You. Isn't
that FUCKED?
Like a missing boy found CoWeRiNg, In the corner,
of his OWN, Room.... Isn't that pathetic,
 in a way?
Whenever I am Bowed in the Apathetic Presence of You, to
Whom every Knee, in **Vaikuntha**, & Tartarus doth,
Bend,
The Mysteries of Nature, the Occult! & our troubled, Schizophrenic
Species, are an open
-Book!

...The Hologram of Louise, Brooks, with
Long hair?
 Is Aiming the sawed off shotgun!! of undying
–Love-
At the wealthy merchants of

-Death-
As they toss only a mere
-Pittance-
To "The Beggars of
- Life",
While the owners of Our Unpopulated,
          store, Day
Dream out of it's Dusty- Window, & wait, impatiently ...... For
A –Customer.....

Thelonious

Monk, had a picture of Billie Holiday taped, On
 To the ceiling, of his
Room,

& Me? I

 Have a picture of –You, TACKED, On to,

Mine.

A Poem Written of the Day Lou Reed Died seems far from "Okay"

It's On days like, "THIS"!!! When
I need, YOU!   The
    Most.

                         When
I wake up hung over, today,
With Yesterdays makeup on my face
           Groaning,
Holding my Liver
To the news that Lou Reed
Has passed over into
The Isle of the Blest as the caressing
Breeze, from the North, disturbs the fresh
Cut, flowers, adorning the
         1914
Era motion picture cameras, constructed,
Out of Bamboo- sticks.

                        When
I feel like an Abstract number in the Bureau
Of statistics, in the midst of the faceless,
unCEAasing hordes,
When I feel like a White,
Oracular, crow, of the porcelain sea,
& everything seems FAR, far
From .."Okay",
      This, is? This,
        IS-

This is Electronic snow Restoring the modesty of
Winters NAKED, bird crowned-Simian haunted,
Tree!
This is, the salient, undeniable fact, that when I went to
School there was only
"One" solar, system, & Pluto! Was still, a, Planet? This, is,
This is a Homosexual gangster rapper in the Bronx
Convicted of Bludgeoning
His neighbor of 24 years, over a 40...cent...debt!
This is, the Heavy petting zoo! & Collapsible picnic kit
& stale myth,
Of Our melodic REVERIE, & we are surviving almost
RELUCTANTLY, with, in,
        It!
When your unsharpened Bayonets! Are being
Thrusted towards
The, The
Obese Leopards leaping out of our enlarged, Pupils! IS
When "I", most ..... Neeeeeed! You, When
Here, &, there! & NOW, &
       ...Then,

       When
6 glass coffins adorn, our wooded hill,
 When an Underage Call girl nervously smoking
         an
Unlit cigarette to the filter, at the
       Center of
The scandal testified, that
Silvio Berlusconi hired, her, &
Other women to perform strip teases in sexy
Nurse, sexy nun! & sexy
Barack Obama...... costumes?
When I feel like the, "LAST OF THE MANY"! & "One
Of the, FEW,"
When the Ayatollah of .... "Parnassus",
Condemns the Democratic Republic of Oceania for
Employing drone attacks, that

Murder countless innocent
civilians, as
A mammoth killing comet lindy hops, Lindy hops
Across our water colored sky, & a Mudslide, thankfully
Hammers a polluted Nudist beach in, "Vancouver", is
When "I", Most!!! Neee
-eeed,
    YOU!

      When
Here, &, There!! &
            ... Now! &...
-Then?
When I feel like, A! Lyric
Without an intricately woven, Harmony,
Or a Familiar, unwanted Refugee,
In my own Fucking Town!!
When I feel like, THE-
When I feel like the shy sister, of an
Extroverted "Family"! or Hannibal,
Hannibal
Son of Hamilcar Barca, square-ing off against the Romans
Shoving peasants speaking "Fluent" gibberish head, first,
Into our Freshly drained, pool, &
The most promiscuous, "Unnaturally seductive",
Of all, Kidnapped women,
Begging the media for Some much needed "Privacy". Are
Being cheated on by the loyalest, most considerate of
All, pregnant, men!
    As the
Wind whipped forest fires, RAGE} While
Horse poisoners in our grey! Swan filled- ocean, are
Swimming side ways in a futile attempt, to
ELUDE that replenishing, infection! When
"Liberty's become a, whore, & we're
all, taking an, Easy Ride, When- When
OUTSIDE!! Of the Modern Utopia stuffed full
Of Tree houses, Igloos?

Loooonggggg Houses, Sand castles! Tee pees! Childrens
        Forts,
"Spanish Style Haciendas"?
& Goya-esque dreams, You are now sitting inside
Of, A
Mysterious, self begotten Woman, wearing a Blonde wig,
Is Struggling to avoid detection in the
Canadian underworld after side stepping
Senescence, & Infiltrating our Bright Future, by entering
Agnostic heaven ALIVE, before the Derailment, as
Wind! Rain! & sea water, devastate the
Northwestern coast as, I sit, on a Grotesquely
Packed shuttle bus, en route to, Visit
My Dad in St. Joseph's Hospital, over hearing the
Most arrogant of Miscreants
Boast about how
Miley Cyrus thinks, Cocaine…. Is!!!!,,,,,, GROSSSSSS

It's On days, like… "THIS", when I, Neee
-eeed!!!! YOU …….. The,

        Most.

CN Tower a.k.a Sergeant Sarah Brown (for Bede)

The C.N tower looks sometimes like a BIG, used,
Hypodermic Needle, with Neon lights!
Full of the loveliest, people, that
On the sad event of my ever becoming
A Heroin addict,
You would fantasize about shooting up,
Into my
ARM,
Like a faded red seduced by it's HILARious,
Birthday, & the blissful antece
-dents, of The best ever summers, to come,
Passing around a dropped, ball, that
Won't bounce back! In the
Supine manner of an unliftable, boulder, rolling
Natural,ly up a steep hill, of plundered
---Silver-
(How was that for an opening, ladies &
Gentlemen & "others"?)

A long deceased grandmother is summoning the
Grandchildren she never met, to come meet
Her beyond the pale of the hungry,
Mouth!
Of her shallow, unmarked grave, &
Crystal beasts!! Of the Chain-sawed, sleep
Walking forest are coveting the alchemistical
Gold of WIZENED fools in full view,
Of gifted vocalists belting out a soulful! Heart
Wrenching tune, on a lip synched- show,

& a vituperative, nymph, whose cold dead
Karla Homolka like eyes, can
Restore full
Sight!! To
The WILFULLY... Blind, My severed, six
Faced head, transforms into
A HUGE Helium inflated balloon orange
Haired Cyborgs pecking
People's 3rd (& 4th) eyes out, with
Their pointy, elongated, Imaginary
BEAKS hold in
Their gloved, limp wristed
Hands as if,
They are... Bodiless sharks & the last,
Navajo Babbler of code lemon stabbing
The armless knife, thrower, accosting my
Treadmills lovers bronze
Man smeared in Red, Ochre, &, WHITE < Clay...

Archaic places, are perishing into modernity Clasping
The last straw that broke the hunched, fabled
Back! Of a PARCHED! Over worked
Camel... Our Donovan Bailey, Usain Bolt
Legged summers are wilt
-ing,
Into the   Past.

A School Bus!
Lugging school kids towards their sterilization
Passes by Me, & everyone on it, (Including the
Bus driver) gives us... The Middle finger...
A Geisha? A sinister geisha wearing
An expensive gangster suit, is travelling to
&, fro, In the summer hail, Sleet, &
-Snow. She
is cloaked in red, night, with chopsticks in her hair,
Repeatedly flashing her tongue... Giving
oral...to the...Air In

Which the skeletal, well moisturized fingers of
a…jealous god(dess) puncture the mammatus
Clouds, to unbuckle
The cotton, emerald studded
Belts! Of
The Queen of the Valkyries, &! The
Daughters of the king, of
The Land(s)
Of…

Octogenarian- YouTH.
being Gas lit, & "catfish
-ed",

By THEIR Bogeymans' RED
Herring,   Crying

…Wolf.

Stair Lifts

Let's dig each other, while we're both,
      "ALIVE",
Let's dig, Dig each other, while
      Lady Luck! Is STILL, on
        "Our" Side,
Let's Dig! Dig each other, while we can still
      Walk!
"Unaided", While our Mobility,
    Is STILL, Unlimited,
While we still possess, Possess the gifts of
Sight! & Sound Let's,
Let's fucking dig one, another, whilst we
Still got all of Our, THICK, Lust
      -rous hair, While
We still have all of our…. TEETH ☺ Let's, Let's
      Dig each other,
Before we need Wheelchairs! "Stair Lifts"! Cane
      Swords &,
"Depend"s, Before we have to Experience
The inevitable transitions of our Family, Ex
-tended family, members,
Associates & Friends! Let's,
      Dig each –other,
Before Cancer! Strokes, & …. Osteoporosis, &
The possible attacks of our Sacred
hearts let's, Dig one
      Another!
Before Alzheimers! Parkinsons, &
      DEMENTIA Before

Cirrhosis of the Liver, Hey! Before
Back problems, "Joint pain", Kidney failure, Diabetes,
    Wrinkles! "Wrinkles" &
        Eventual Decay,
           O god!
Katie, I know something Better lays "Beyond" You know
    "Something" Bet
        -ter lays
Beyond but let's, Dig, Dig each other,
Before Someone Prettier! Sexier! Younger, Funnier?
Cooler! Smarter, EXOTIC,
Richer, & a better dancer comes along
      Let's!
Let's Dig one
ANOTHER< Before
    World war
         3?
No matter what assails "Us" up ahead,
No matter our vile, or golden fate,
Before Anubis, Osiris, "Ammit?" the next Pandemic, & Our
Lost saints AWAIT, Dig, Meeee
      -ee, while
 We still possess the recipe, for the seed/
Salt of,
Platinum & Gold! While
We can still witness, the Beautiful colors of the
Chain sawed, sleep
Walking forests
   In Your, flask!!?
      Dig ME!
Despite Ebola! Tainted sustenance, COERCION, The global
Housing Crisis, the increasing vicissitudes, man made,
Micro organisms &
The encroaching enGNARL-ment, Dig!
ME,
Despite the malefactors, Psychopaths, creeps, & other Para
-sites Ruling our Planet,
& Mutant strains of the Flu….. Despite, the Frankensteins

of intelligence agencies,& the cruel, In

-humane Folly, & MASS distraction,

Despite BEACHED WHALES, the changing of the climate,
    & the spirits of

Drowned Women, who Bewitch, & DROWN,

Lonesome passing, men?

Despite the catalogue of Horrors, MY insecurities, & feelings of
    Worthlessness,

MY fear of Rejection & getting hurt, YOUR

Self doubt, & anxiety, &

The Seemingly unENDing, Degrading bloody
    Hassle,

Despite packed subway trains at rush hour, &

Walking, Leafless! Snow covered trees,

& The Million, "Advertisements", attempting to make us
    Feel,

    "Inadequate".

Let's Dig, Dig each-other!! While we are, Both!
    "ALIVE"

Let's Dig, One another, Whilst Lady Luck!
    LADY, LUCK, is, still, on
      "Our"……Side…

Don Octavio DeFlores

Since everything has already seemingly
Been said,
What can I tell you, huh, that you haven't
Already, heard?
What can I say, My love, that a hundred
Other poets, philosophers, Madmen, Drunkards, Don
Juans, Tedious Ideologues,
& Psychologists haven't, already
Told you?

What if I showed, You,
Pluto lingering across the sky
From the Black, Lactating
Sun,
At Midnight?
What If I showed you Homosexual gangster
rappers licking Vaginas, that
Have red wine stained
Teeth?
or Passable transgender women carrying water guns
full of
Whiskey, bullying MEAN Lesbians,
Astride a soiled Dove?
Ink black Caucasians rowing dragon
Boats through Wooden
Water?
Super effeminate misogynists wearing pink crop tops
That say
"If you think I'm a BITCH, wait until you meet my

Mother" ;)
Or FREED NEGROES,
Synchronizing 70's porno, to .....MUSIC?
A Congested city, blowing it's
Snotty nose?
& a feral kitten attacking, it's own White -shadow,
On Our curved, load bearing wall?
What if I told you I Could (without fail, Hesitation,
Or remorse) engineer the "Liquidation"
Of the 5 crime families Of
New YORK, & the One,
In Montreal, & do to my friendly enemies, What
Duke Valentino did to Vitellozzo Vitelli, Oliverotto
Da Fermo & Company,
At Sinigaglia, & notify you about
My years working at A "Grow-op", & dealing Ecstasy
After I dropped out of school, & really mean it ?
Would You believe me? Would "That"
...Do?
What If I were to Tell you that We are
Before "A"! & after....
Z?
& that we always "Were", & will always
.... Be?
When Every Illusion/ Delusion ceased to Fascinate!
& Soothe Me,
When every Friday, & Saturday night "Ceased
To be a Joy",
& Even my Favorite foods began to lose
Their taste,
& "My world of dreams, seemed Bare",
You appeared, There,
"Beyond the pair of Opposites" like a Wilderness
Blooming!!
In a Continent, of Liquid, speckled, Philosophic
....Stone, I'm,
I'm like a Quixotic Knight bending
My knee in the reverent service

Of My Shy,
Bold eyed Lady where the protective, walls,
Of Melting, Ice!
Meets "The Grail Castle", (of sand) by the
Sea, As the Full moon (during an Eclipse) Rises
Over the Tranquil fields, of the Impaled,
& Thousands of Lifeless sea creatures
wash ashore in, Nova scotia,
How's That?

What if I "Toldt" you that it is
"Transition or Glory" for us two
who, who
are swinging for the Fences
of –Posterity- (Insert your name Here)
Carlo Gambino, Meyer Lansky or, NOTHING, for
Us now….. it
Is?
I'll tell you how It, is,
I'll befriend & tame every Inner Demon, for real, Slay! &
…Sip
The Blue, blood, of every Dragon, Wake every Sleeping
Giant & Dog where they lay, & Tease out
FACT,
From every supposition in the untouristed Land,
Where the dead are considered "Lucky",
& the Mute Banshees, have long stopped Scream
-ing,
because "What's the Point?"
I will sing you! (Insert your name here)As no one ELSE, has ever
sought, or imagined
To have sung you!
For you, I will Run! Hop! Skip, Slither, Cart
Wheel, Jump!!
For you I will sit upon the Stumps of
Walking!
Leafless! Snow covered trees
Consigned, to the Wood chipper, & Lament

The Vanishing honey bee, & the encroaching,
EnGNARLment, & "Bet
The Farm"
For You I Promise to "Joyfully Participate in the
Sorrows of THIS World",
like the Exemplification of the "Thrillingly promiscuous Fusion",
& Be like Crystal beasts! Of the chain sawed
Forest or "the Noon Day Sun" (at midnight) Climbing toward it's
ZENITH,
& Repart the red sea while Pushing
Everything TOO, far,

I will Show you who, the "Moustache petes" caging
Us in the Lower chakras as
A Species, are, I can show you, who, who
The schoolyard bullies of the world, are!
If you'll let me?
But that rhythm sounds familiar! I've already done that.
No?
I'll Tell You all about Strung out Models,
Models!
Brit-tle Gaunt-men....& a
Poisoned, Lean! Feather
-less, wrought iron Eagle being Bled,
White!
By a Lurking, Faceless Man,
Caressing Wind sculpted
Rock!
& Liquid Metal, ornately .... Wrought! I can
see your Damp, footsteps soft Im
-print, eva-porat-ing,
from the glossy surface of the shift-ing, garbage
Littered-Sand,
I can Glimpse Your Ubiquitous, Scarcely
Legible insignia, everywhere I
Turn,
What If I told You I once Witnessed your
Ever altering, self replicating

Form
Emanating from the aether,
Hovering over our Hyperkinetic, Blue
Lotus Blossom Shaped city
Like a Giant!
Bright Green BUBBLE, float
-ing,
(Benevolently)
over our former empires, De-ci-mat-ed
.....Rubble?

(Insert Your Name here)
Should I say things that we all feel,
But never shout aloud,
Like "FUCK YOUUUUUUUUU
Scotia Bank, I'm DEFINITELY not, Richer
Than I think, nor
in fact, is ANYONE I KNOW",
If we are talking about finances (of course)
If It is truly impossible, to say something new,
Then I am doomed, forever, it seems, to give Fascinating,
"Muscular "variations, interpretations of the well worn, iron clad
themes,
Fantasies, Philosophies, nightmares,
& ... Dreams, & need not
worry?

(Insert your name here)
Interknit your hidden face, with
Mine!
Heighten our every waking moment,
Into a PEAK experience, Stop Forced Organ harvesting,
 In China, Grant Victory!! To those battling
"Erectile Dysfunction", &
CANCER,
Cure Male Pattern Baldness, & Dementia,
In Women &,
Men,

Help feed Toronto's Feral Cats,
& Help, Keep the TTC
Safe,
"End This Day, what the Ides of March
Began!"
& give us ALL yet, another, tiny glimpse 'tween the lavender
curtains concealing the structural, Reality,
behind the Wagner-ian Stage-set.....

I only undertook the writing of this poem
To tell you "Something",
That you haven't already
Heard,
I wanted to write you this poem on biodegradable paper,
Made out
of the worlds oldest, largest living
tree~!
I undertook the futile, Herculean task of Conjuring this
Here poem to try, to tell You
"Something", Something that a Hundred other
Poets, Philosophers, Madmen! Drunkards, Players,
Tedious Ideologues, Rhetoricians
& Psychologists haven't ALREADY, told
You. But
what!
Can I possibly tell you, Huh!? You... You
Whose probably heard,
It - ALL?

April 30th, 2020

Like the gnarled Dissipate,
                of "the Spirits awful Night"

On the Small love seat,
               of some SHRILL,
       Benevolent
 Harpy,

I am
Awakened, Rudely, By the Crystallization of the
Passage of
        -Time

In the emblematic form,
          of a disgruntled,
               Male
Roommate, taking a grisly, Thunderous!
Nauseating piss, in their Communal, Dish filled
…. Sink….

I Know what you think,
       I know,
Exactly what you are thinking, Dear reader,
       Sweet companion!

I know you are wondering how,
How after living like a crowned prince
             for
More than a decade, & a day, Did

The oriental Rug get pulled out from under Me,
& My life get 360'd thus

causing Me to wake up ..HERE,
        (huh?) Now?
How,
How Could "I", after spending a blissfully iniquitous
                Night,
In what can only be inadequately described as "Ecstatic
Flight?" awake to such a horrific scene?

I dunno,
        I don't, know,

THINE guess,
            is as good as
  mine, man.....

It could be A LOT worse,
        I could NOT, Have 2 vials Left
Of whatever it was,
 I was flying on last night,
Stashed, into My grey,
& Black, argyle
Sock,

The Hot, coagulated light, from the midnight sun could
NOT,
Be Hemorrhaging Through Her California Shutters
Into a puddle, on their dirty,
                        un-carpet ed Floor,
It could be ALOT ....worse. though,
        Believe me!
Because it has,

I Could NOT,
        Have a sensitive,
Damn near heroic bottle, of Red wine

to ease
My precarious transition, into
                    The,
 New day,

It could Be A LOT worse,
        Though, I could
NOT,
Be having dinner with a SENSUAL,
        Sophisticated Lady
at her place,
            in a few, hours,
But Still!
… For some Obscure reason,

As I begin My Ascent from Crow,
     to Raven,
                to -Phoenix?
Through Vitality & Decay! &,…….
Back!
As Fact becomes

"Fiction" & Fiction becomes

"Fact"

I can't Help, but!   FEEL,

Like the gnarled, dissipate!
     of "The Spirits awful
Night!"

Being crudely, awakened, By the crystallization, of
The Passage
Of

……….-Time……

List of Poetry Readings & Essential Appearances by Stedmond pardy

100,000 POETS FOR CHANGE
(with Pat Connors, Dane Sawn, Marsha Barber, Georgia Wilder, Brenda Clews, Luciano Iacobelli, Charles C. Smith, & Donna Langevin)
Hirut Restaurant, September 23rd, 2019
Toronto, Ont.

Art Bar Poetry Series
(With Brenda Clews, & Adebe D,A)
Freetimes café, July 9th, 2019
Toronto, Ont.

Ian Ferrier's Words & Music Show
June 30th, 2019
Casa Del Popolo Montreal, Quebec.

The Salon of the Collective creative
(with Lisa de Nikolitis, Ruth Zuchter, Peter Graham, & Nancy Ceneviva)
Annette Street Library
Toronto, Ont.

Shab-er- Sher Nowruz Celebration
(With Jade Wallace, Padideh Ahrarnejad and Ali Massoud)
Tranzac Club, March 26th. 2019
Toronto, Ont.

Secret Handshake Gallery readings
(with Kate DE jong, David Roche, George Zancola)
October 28th, 2019 , Toronto, ont.

YTGA July open mic at studio.89
July 29th, 2018
Studio 89. Mississauga, Ont.

Love Poetry Festival
(with bill bissett, George Elliot Clarke, Catherine
Graham, Michelle Alfano, Domenico Capilongo,
Banoo zan, James Daehle, & Norma Linder)
Queen Books, July 28th, 2018, Toronto, ont.

Wild Writers Poetry Series
(With Adebe D.A) May, 1st, 2018
Poetry jazz Café, Toronto, Ont.

One man reading at "the Cineforum"
The Cineforum, September 30th, 2017
Toronto Ont.

Brenda Clews' Poetry & music salon
Fundraiser fort Mcmurray Fire Disaster
Palmerston Library, May 31st, 2016
Toronto, Ont.

Howl 89.5 Ciut Radio
(with Valentino Assenza, & Spencer Butt)
May 18th, 2016

Wild Writers poetry series
(With Ellen Jaffe)
Poetry jazz café ,july 12th, 2017
Toronto, Ont.

Everett Poetry night
Café zippy, April 20th, 2017
Everett Washington, USA

Dirty Laundry Poetry Series
(with Derkson Dalton, Whitney French,
& Zak Jones) Nov.12th, 2016.
Toronto, Ont.

Art Bar Poetry series
(With Roger Greenwall, & Stephanie Yorke)
September 28th, 2016
Freetimes café, Toronto, Ont.

Wild writers Poetry series
(With Myna Wallin)
Poetry jazz café, March 30th, 2016
Toronto, Ont.

Brenda Clews' Poetry Salon
(with Kevin Fortnum & Amoeba Starfish)
Urban Gallery. Feb.28th. 2015
Toronto, Ont.

Art bar Poetry series
(With Max Layton & Benjamin Hackman)
Black swan tavern, March 24th, 2015)

Howl at the Q-space
(With Nik Beat, Norman Allan, & Laura L'Rock)
The Q-space, April 11th, 2013
Toronto, Ont.

One man Reading at "The Cineforum"
March 15th, & 22nd, 2013
Toronto, Ont.

Record vault Reading
(with NIk Beat, Brandon Pitts. Laura DeLeon,
Vanessa McGowan, & Laura L'Rock)
The Record vault, October 28th, 2012
Toronto, Ont.

Gadist Poetry Reading
(With Brandon Pitts, & Nik Beat)
Sonic Café, May 27th, 2012
Toronto, Ont.

Howl 89.5 Ciut radio
(with Nik Beat, Saskia Van teetering)
April 4th, 2012

Biographical Note

Stedmond Pardy is a self educated, Left handed Poet of Mixed Ancestry (Newfoundland & St.Kitts/Nevis). Originally from the Lakeshore, Mimico area, & Now residing ...Dionysus knows Where?.... He got into the literary scene after the music Reviewer The Mysterious Lonely Vagabond, got hold of some of his work, & Hooked him up with The late great poet, & Host of the radio show "Howl – CIUT 89.5FM", Since then He has Performed his work Around the Greater Toronto Area, & has appeared on stages In Montreal, & Washington State. The Quotes "An artist is an instrument through which the Universe reveals itself" & "Word poetry Is for every man, but soul poetry, alas, Is not Heavily distributed", Are the words he tries To live by.